THE FIRST DISCIPLINE
of the
UNITED AMERICAN FREE WILL BAPTISTS

Written under the direction of
THE GENERAL CONFERENCE

SIXTH REVISION

Approved by
THE GENERAL CONFERENCE
AT KINSTON, N.C.

1999

THE FIRST DISCIPLINE
OF THE
UNITED AMERICAN FREE WILL BAPTISTS

Written Under The Direction of
THE GENERAL CONFERENCE

SIXTH REVISION

APPROVED
BY THE GENERAL CHURCH
AT KINSTON, NC

1999

PUBLISHED BY THE
UNITED AMERICAN FREE WILL BAPTIST
DENOMINATION INCORPORATED
KINSTON, NORTH CAROLINA, USA

AUGUST 2019

BISHOP J. E. REDDICK
GENERAL BISHOP

Table of Contents

UNITED AMERICAN FREE WILL BAPTIST DENOMINATION, INC.

Discipline Revision Committee
1999

Mr. Thomas D. Adam
Dr. Billie Anderson
Mrs. Ella Armstrong
Mrs. Carrie U. Best
Mrs. Thelma E. Best
Dr. W.J. Best
Mr. O'Berry Bizzell
Mrs. Beatrice Chapman
*Mr. Peter Dockery
Bishop Robert Douglas
Ms. Loree Durham
Bishop G.A. Fountain
Mrs. Katie Forshee
Bishop J.N. Gilbert
Bishop M.L. Gore
Dr. Robert Gorham
Mr. Frederick Graham
Mr. Clarence Hicks
Mrs. Georgia Jackson
Mrs. Rita Jackson Gilbert
Mr. LaDarius M. Jefferson
Mr. Frank Jones
Mrs. Rosalie Jones
Eldress Sarah King
Dr. Rhuarma Knox

Elder Douglas Kornegay
Mr. W.A. Lawson, Sr.
Mrs. Ernestine Leach
Mrs. Jean Lee
Bishop Theodore McAllister, Jr.
*Bishop M.N. McLean
Mrs. Eva M. Minter
Dr. W.H. Mitchell
Bishop C.R. Parker
Elder J.W. Peek
Mr. Moses Ramsey
Mr. Curtis Raye
Mrs. Thelma Reddick
Eldress Mildra Ross
*Mrs. Mattie Thompson
Bishop Bobbie Vereen
Elder J.H. Vines
*Eldress Mary Wallace
Dr. Michael Whitfield
Elder J.L. Wilson
Mr. Samuel Wilson
*Elder J.H. Wilkes
Mr. Charles Winston
Bishop J.E. Reddick

(* = deceased members)

The Roll of General Moderators and General Bishops of the United American Free Will Baptist Denomination, Incorporated

- Moderator W.H. Hodges

- Moderator Ramson Becton

- Moderator E.M. Hill

- Moderator H.R. Reaves

- Moderator O.L. Williams

- Bishop R.D. Pridgen

- Bishop W.L. Jones

- Bishop W.H. Mitchell

- Bishop J.E. Reddick

Preface

In keeping with an assignment given by the United American Free Will Baptist Denomination for the revision of the Book of Discipline, a committee was appointed to fulfill this task. After several meetings, involving much prayer and discussion, the committee recommended some changes and alterations for the book to meet today's time. Thus, we give our denomination a written document by which every member should be governed.

The Book of Discipline shall prescribe laws and regulations to govern our churches as well as the annexes of the General Church; the Home Mission, Sunday School, Young People's Christian League, Ushers, and General Departments.

If we are to be a united church, the committee feels that these rules must be obeyed by every member of this denomination. We further maintain, that no member of the church, regardless of position or title, is exempted from these rules.

The Book of Discipline is the governing guide for the United American Free Will Baptist Denomination, Incorporated and is the prescribing source of laws and regulations to govern our member churches and all annexes of the General Church; the Home Mission, Sunday School, Young People's Christian League, and General Departments.

All members, regardless of position or title, are held accountable to the obedience of the Book of Discipline.

Special Note

Be it understood that anytime a masculine pronoun is used or referred to in this publication, it is done so in a nominative case, which includes females.

Our Faith

1. We believe that there is but one living, true and eternal God the Father, of whom all things, from everlasting to everlasting, glorious and immutable in all His attributes.—I Corinthians 8:6; Isaiah 40:28.

2. We believe that there is one Lord Jesus Christ, by whom are all things, the only begotten Son of God, born of the Virgin Mary, whom God freely sent into this world because of the great love wherewith He loved the world, and Christ as freely gave Himself a ransom for all, tasting death for every man; who was buried and rose again the third day, and ascended into Heaven, from whence we look for Him, the second time, in the clouds of Heaven, at the last day, to judge both quick and dead. I Timothy 2:15, 6; Hebrews 2:9; I John 2:2; Revelation 1:7; Acts 24: 15.

3. We believe that there is one Holy Ghost, the precious gift of the Father, through His dear Son, unto the world, who quickeneth and draweth sinners home to God. — John 3:17; Acts 2:4; Ephesians 4:4,5,6.

4. We believe that in the beginning God made man upright and placed him in a state of glory without sin, from which he voluntarily, by transgression, fell, and by that means brought on himself a miserable and mortal state, subject to death. — Genesis 2:17; 3:17,18,19.

5. We believe that God is not willing that any should perish, but that all should come to repentance and the knowledge of the truth, that they might be saved, for which end Christ hath commanded the Gospel to be preached among nations and to every

creature.— Mark 6:15; Luke 24:47.

6. We believe that no man shall suffer in hell for want of Christ that died for him, but, as the Scripture has said, for denying the Lord that bought them, because they believe not in the name of the only begotten Son of God. Unbelief, therefore, being the cause why the just and righteous God of Heaven will condemn the children of men, it follows, against all contradiction, that all men at one time or other, are found in such a capacity as that through the grace of God they may be eternally saved.— 2 Peter 2:1; I John I: 17; Acts 17:3; Mark 6:6; Hebrews 3:10; I John 5:10.

7. We believe the whole Scriptures are infallibly true, and that they are the only rules of faith and practice.

8. We believe in the doctrine of general provision made of God in Christ for the benefit of all mankind who repent and believe the Gospel.—Luke 14:16, 20.

9. We believe that sinners are drawn to God the Father by the Holy Ghost through Christ, His Son, and that the Holy Ghost offers His divine aid to all the human family, should they give place to His divine teaching; whereas such who do not receive the divine impressions of His Holy Spirit shall, at a future day, own their condemnation just and charge themselves with their own damnation for willfully rejecting the offers of sovereign grace.—Matthew 11:27.

10. We believe that men, not considered simply as men, but ungodly men, who turned the grace of God into lasciviousness, denying the only Lord God, and our Lord Jesus Christ that brought them. Shall bring upon themselves swift destruction; but we observe that they, and such as the Apostle saith;

because they receive not the love of the truth, that they might be saved; therefore, the indignation and wrath of God is upon every soul of man that doth evil, living and dying, for there is no respect of persons with God.—Jude 1:4.

11. We believe that all children dying in infancy having not actually transgressed against the law of God in their own persons, are only subject is the first death, which was brought upon them by the fall of the first Adam, and not anyone of them dying in that state shall suffer punishment in hell by the guilt of Adam's sin, for of such is the kingdom of Heaven.—Matthew 19:14.

12. We believe that good works are the fruits of a saving faith, and that in the use of the means of grace, and not out of the use of these means, eternal life is promised to men.— Revelation 22:14, 15.

13. We believe that no man has any warrant in the Holy Scriptures for justification before God through his own works, power or ability which he has in and of himself, only as he by grace is made able to come to God, through Jesus Christ, believing the righteousness of Jesus Christ to be imputed to all believers for their eternal acceptance with God.—Romans 4:24.

14. We believe that all things are predestined in the wisdom of God, so that God knoweth whatsoever can or cannot come to pass upon all supposed conditions, yet not as having decreed any person to everlasting death or everlasting life out of respect of mere choice; further, that He hath appointed the godly unto life and the ungodly, who die in sin, unto death. — Hebrews 4:13.

15. We believe as touching Gospel Ordinances, in believer's baptism, laying on of the hands, receiving of the sacrament in bread and wine, washing the saint's feet, anointing the sick with oil in the name of the Lord, fasting, praying, singing praises to God, and the public ministry of the Word, with every institution of the Lord we shall find in the New Testament.—Luke 22 19, 20.

16. We believe the Gospel mode of baptism is by immersion, and that the believers are the only subjects for baptism. Matthew 3:8-16.

17. We believe in the general resurrection of the dead and the final judgment at the last day.— John 5:28, 29.

18. We believe the happiness of the righteous is eternal and the torments of the wicked are endless—Matthew 25:46.

19. We believe in the complete development of the whole man. Mind, body, and soul. In order to achieve this we believe in the instructions of the Apostle Paul as recorded in 2 Timothy 2: 15.

20. We believe that the world is God's mission field and that we are commanded of Him to "go therefore into all the world proclaiming the good news of the kingdom of God."—Matthew 28:18; St. John 10:16.

21. We believe in the Scriptural methods of supporting God's work. This includes tithing, free will offerings, and service.—I Corinthians 9: 14; Malachi 2:8-10; I John 3:17.*

*All Scriptural references used in this book are from the King James Version of the Bible.

1. **THE SCRIPTURES**—The Scriptures of the Old and New Testament were given by inspiration of God, and are binding on all as our only infallible rule of faith and practice.

2. **GOD**—There is only one living and true God, infinite in all His attributes—the Creator, Preserver and Governor of the universe—revealed to us in the Scriptures, as the Father, the Son, and the Holy Ghost.

3. **CHRIST**—He is God manifested in the flesh-being in His divine nature true God, in His human nature true Man, united in the person of the Messiah or Mediator for the redemption of the world.

4. **THE HOLY GHOST**—He possesses all personal divine attributes, being the reprover, comforter, and sanctifier of man.

5. **DIVINE PURPOSES AND PROVIDENCE**—The purposes of God are eternal and immutable; His wise and holy Providence is over all beings and in all things to secure His own glory and the highest welfare of His creatures.

6. **ORIGINAL STATE AND FALL OF MAN**—Man was created upright but by disobedience, fell into a state of condemnation. All succeeding generations inherit this fallen nature, therefore all men are alienated from God. There is no salvation from his guilt and the power of sin, except through God's redeeming grace.

7. **THE ATONEMENT**—Christ in His great compassion offered Himself a sacrifice in our stead, and thus by His life, sufferings and death made an atonement

which is full and free to us all, and opens the only way of salvation.

8. **GRACE**—No one can by his own work or merit obtain salvation, which is wholly of the grace of God, and through which all spiritual blessings are bestowed upon us.

9. **CONDITIONS OF SALVATION**—These are repentance, implying Godly sorrow for wrongdoing; open confession and utter renunciation of sin. Faith is the unreserved commital of the mind and heart to receive, obey, and trust Christ; and regeneration by the Holy Spirit, whereby the 50U] iS freed from the dominion of sin and brought into the glorious liberty of the children of God.

10. **ELECTION**—God has not fixed the future state of men by any unconditional decree, but determined from the beginning to save all who should comply with the conditions of salvation.

11. **PERSEVERANCE**—None will be finally saved but those who through grace, persevere in holiness to the end.

12. **SALVATION FREE**—God desires the salvation of all, the Gospel invites all, the Holy Ghost strives with all, and whosoever will may come and take the water of life freely.

13. **FREEDOM OF THE WILL**—The human will is not controlled by any fatal necessity or external force, but is free and self-determined, having power to yield to gracious influences and live, or restrain them and perish.

14. **GOSPEL ORDINANCES**—Baptism or the immersion of believers in water, and the Lord's Supper, and the washing of the Saint's feet, are ordinances to be perpetuated under the Gospel of universal

obligations, and to be administered to all true believers.

15. **THE SABBATH**—The Christian Sabbath is a divine institution, binding on all, and should be observed by abstaining from secular business and amusement, and consecrated to the worship of God and spiritual improvements.

16. **THE RESURRECTION, FINAL JUDGMENT AND FUTURE RETRIBUTION**—Christ will make His second appearance at the end of the world, when the dead will be raised, the judgment set, the righteous be received to eternal blessedness and the wicked to endless sufferings.

Church Covenant

Having given ourselves to God through Jesus Christ, and adopted the preceding articles as our confession of faith, we now give ourselves to each other by the will of God, and agree to the following Church Covenant:

1. We solemnly covenant, before God, that we will strive, by His assisting grace, to exemplify our profession by a corresponding practice. We covenant and agree, as members of the Church and as Christians to watch over each other in love for mutual upbuilding in Gospel faith, endeavoring to keep the unity of the spirit in the bond of peace, to be careful of each other's reputation, to confess our faults one to another, to strengthen the feeble and kindly admonish the erring, and to labor together for the building up of the Church and the denomination, and the salvation of sinners.

2. We promise that we will faithfully and constantly

maintain secret and family prayer, and religiously instruct those under our care.

3. We covenant and agree to use our influence to sustain the regular public worship of God, contributing according to our ability and circumstances for the support of our ministry and other Church expenses among us; that we will be benevolent to the needy, especially to the poor of our own Church.

4. We promise that, so far as we shall be able, we will attend public worship, the social meetings of the Church, and report ourselves regularly at the quarterly conferences, and that we will walk in all the ordinances of the Lord's house.

5. We covenant and agree that we will abstain from all vain amusements and sinful conformity to the world; that we will not traffic in, use, nor furnish to others, drugs, intoxicating drinks as a beverage and that we will sustain the benevolent enterprises of our denomination and the Church, as missions, education, Sabbath schools, moral reforms, and all others which tend to the glory of God and the welfare of man.

And may the God of peace sanctify us holy, and preserve us blameless unto the coming of our Lord Jesus Christ, that we may join the glorified around the throne of God in ascribing blessings, and honor, and power, and glory to Him that sitteth on the throne and unto the precious Lamb forever. Amen.

Affirmation of Faith

We believe that God is the Father Almighty and that He is maker of Heaven and earth as the Scriptures have said. We believe in Jesus, that He is the Christ and is the only begotten Son of the Father. He is the way, the truth, and the life. He was conceived by the Holy Ghost, born of the Virgin Mary, suffered under Pontius Pilate, was crucified, dead and buried. On the third day, He rose from the dead and declared victory over the grave, death, and hell. He has gone back to the Father to prepare a place for us in His Kingdom. He will come back as He promised to judge the world and to deliver the righteous. We believe in the Holy Ghost, the Christian Church, the Communion of Saints, the forgiveness of sins, the resurrection of the body, and eternal life for all true believers.
Amen.

The Holy Scriptures

These are the Old and New Testaments; they were written by holy men, inspired by the Holy Spirit, and contain God's revealed will to man. They are sufficient and infallible guides in religious faith and practice.

Being and Attributes of God

The Scriptures teach that there is only one true and living God' who is a Spirit[2], Self-existing[3], Eternal[4], Immutable[5], Omnipresent[6], Omniscient[7], Omnipotent[8], Independent[9], Good[10], Wise[11], Holy[12].

1. Deuteronomy 6:4, The Lord our God is one Lord. I Corinthians 8:14, There is none other God but one; Jeremiah 10: 10, But the Lord is the true God, He is the living God. John 7:28; 2 Corinthians 1: 18; 1 John 5 :20; I Timothy 6: 17.

2. John 4:24, God is Spirit: 2 Corinthians 3:17.

3. Exodus 3:14, And God said unto Moses; I am that I am. Psalm 83:18; John 5:26; Revelation 1:4.

4. Psalm 90:2, From everlasting to everlasting thou art God. Deuteronomy 33:27; Isaiah 57:15; Romans 1:20; I Timothy 1:17.

5. Malachi 3:6, For I am the Lord, I change not. Numbers 23:18; James 1:17.

6. 1 Kings 8:27, But will God indeed dwell on the earth? Behold, the heaven of heavens cannot contain thee. Jeremiah 23:24; Psalm 139:7-19; Isaiah 57:15; Acts 18:24.

7. Acts 15:18, Known unto God are all his works from the beginning of the world. I Chronicles 28:9; Psalm 9:49, 10; Acts I :24.

8. Revelation 19:6, The Lord God omnipotent reigneth. Job 42:2; Psalm 135:6; Matthew 19:26; Mark 14:35; Luke 18:27.

9. Ephesians 4:6, One God and Father of all, who is above all. Job 9:12; Isaiah 14:12, 14; Daniel 4:35;

Romans 11:33-36.

10. Psalm 119:68, Thou are good, and doest good. Psalm 25:8; 106:1; 145:9; Matthew 19:17.

11. Romans 16:27, To God only wise, be glory through Jesus Christ forever. Daniel 2:20; I Timothy 1:17; Jude 25.

12. Leviticus 19:2, I the Lord your God am holy. Job 6:10.

Just', and merciful[2], the Creator[3], Preserver[4], and Governor[5], of the universe; the Redeemer[6], Saviour[7], Sanctifier[8], and Judge[9] of men; and the only proper object of worship[10]. The mode of His existence, however, is a subject far above the understanding of men"—finite beings cannot comprehend Him[12]. There is nothing in the universe that can justly represent Him, for there is none like Him[13]. He is the fountain of all perfection and happiness. He is glorified by the whole creation, and is worthy to be loved and served by all intelligence[14].

1. Deuteronomy 32:4, Just and right is he. Psalms 92:15; 119:137; Zephaniah 3:5.

2. Ephesians 2:4, God, who is rich in mercy. Exodus 34:6; Nehemiah 9:17; Psalm 100:5.

3. Genesis 1:1, in the beginning God created the heaven and the earth. Exodus 20:11; Psalm 33:6 9; Colossians 1:16; Hebrews 11:3.

4. Nehemiah 9:6,Thou preservest them all. Job 7:20; Colossians 1:17; Hebrews 1:3.

5. Psalm 47:7, God is the King of all the earth. 2 Chronicles 20:6; Psalm 95:3.

6. Isaiah 47:4, As for our Redeemer, the Lord of hosts is his name. Psalm 78:35; Proverbs 23:11; Isaiah 41:14;59:20;Jeremiah 50:34.

7. Isaiah 45:21, A just God and a Saviour. Isaiah 43:3-

11; 49:26.

8. Exodus 31:13, I am the Lord that doth sanctify you. I Thessalonians 5:23; Jude 1.

9. Hebrews 12:23, God the Judge of all. Genesis 18:25; Psalm 50:6; 2 Timothy 4:8.

10. Exodus 34:14, Thou shalt worship no other god. Exodus 20:4, 5; Matthew 4:10; Revelation 19:10.

11. Job 11:7, Canst thou by searching find out God? Isaiah 40;28.

12. Romans 11:33, How unsearchable are his judgments, and his ways past finding out. Job 26:14.

13. Exodus 9:14, There is none other like me in all the earth. Exodus 8:10; I Chronicles 17:20.

14. Psalm 19:1, 2, The heavens declare the glory of God; and the firmament sheweth his handywork. Day unto day uttereth speech, and night unto night sheweth knowledge. Psalm 145:10, All thy works shall praise thee. Psalm 150:6, Let everything that hath breath praise the Lord.

Divine Government and Providence

1. God exercises a providential care and superintendency over all his Creatures[1]. And governs the world in wisdom and mercy, according to the testimony of His Word[2].

2. God has endowed man with power of free choice, and governs him by moral laws and motives; and this power of free choice is the exact measure of man's responsibility[3].

3. All events are present with God from everlasting to everlasting; but His knowledge of them does not in any sense cause them, nor does He decree all events which He knows will occur[4].

16

1. **OF THE WORLD.** God created the world, and all things that it contains, for His own pleasure and glory and the enjoyment of His creatures[5].

[1]Acts 17:28, in Him we live, and move, and have our being. Matthew 10:30, The very hairs of your head are all numbered. Psalm 104:13, 14; Job 14:5; Ephesians 1:11.
[2]Psalm 22:28, For the kingdom is the LORD'S; and he is the governor among the nations. Psalm 97:2, Righteousness and judgment are the habitation of his throne. Isaiah 33:22; Exodus 34:6; Job 36:5.
[3]Deuteronomy 30: 19,1 have set before you life and death, blessing and cursing; therefore choose life, that both thou and thy seed may live. Isaiah 1:18-20; John 5:40; Romans 2:14, 15; Proverbs I :24-28.
[4]Ezekiel 33:11, As I live, saith the Lord GOD, I have no pleasure in the death of the wicked; but that the wicked turn from his way and live. Acts 14:18; I Samuel 2:30; Ezekiel 18:20 25, 31; Jeremiah 44:4.
[5]Revelation 4:11, Thou hast created all things, and for thy pleasure they are and were created. Isaiah 43:7; I Timothy 6:17, The living God, who giveth us richly of all things to enjoy.

2. **OF THE ANGELS.** The angels were created by God[1] to glorify Him[2] and obey Hiscommandments[3]. Those who have kept their first estate He employs in ministering blessings to the heirs of salvation[4] and in executing His judgments upon the world[5].

3. **OF MAN.** God created man, consisting of a material

body and a thinking, rational soul[6]. He was made in the image of God, to glorify his Maker[7].

Primitive State of Man, And His Fall

Our first parents, in their original state, were upright. They naturally preferred and desired to obey their Creator, and had no preference or desire to transgress His will[8] until they were influenced and inclined by the tempter to disobey God's commands. Previous to this, the only tendency of their nature was to do righteousness. In consequence of the first transgression, the state under which the posterity of Adam came into the world is so different from that of Adam that they have not that righteousness and purity which Adam had before the fall; they are not willing to obey God, but are inclined to evil[1]. Hence none, by virtue of any natural goodness and mere work of their own, can become the children of God[2]; but they are all dependent for salvation upon the redemption effected through the blood of Christ, and upon being created anew unto obedience through the operation of the Spirit[3]; both of which are freely provided for every descendant of Adam[1].

[1]Colossians 1: 16, For by him were all things created, that are in heaven, and that are in earth, visible and invisible
[2]Revelation 7: 11, And all the angels stood around about. . .and fell before the throne on their faces, and worshipped God.
[3]Psalm 103:20, Bless the LORD, ye his angels...that do his commandments.
[4]Hebrews 1:14, Are they not all ministering spirits, sent forth to minister for them who shall be heirs of salvation? Jude 6.
[5]2 Samuel 24:16, The angel stretched forth out his hand

upon Jerusalem to destroy it. Revelation 16:1.
[6]Genesis 2:7, And the LORD God formed man of the dust of the ground, and breathed into his nostrils the breath of life; and man became a living soul.
[7]Genesis 1:27, so God created man in his own image, in the image of God created he him. I Corinthians 6:20.
[8]Ecclesiastes 7:29, God hath made man upright. Ephesians 4:24; Colossians 3:10.

The Christ

Jesus Christ, the Son of God, possesses all divine perfections. As He and the Father are one, He is His divine nature, filled all the offices and performed the works of God to His creatures that have been the subjects of revelations to us. As man, He performed all the duties toward God that we are required to perform, repentance of sin excepted.
His divinity is proved from His titles. His attributes, and His works.

[1]Psalm 51:5, Behold, I was shapen in iniquity; and in sin did my mother conceive me. Romans 8:7, The carnal mind is enmity against God. Ephesians 2:3, And were by nature the children of wrath, even as others. Psalm 58:3; Genesis 8:21; John 3:6; Galatians 5:19-21; Romans 5:1 2.
[2]John 6:44, No man can come to me, except the Father which hath sent me draw him. I Corinthians 2:14, The natural man receiveth not the things of the Spirit of God; for they are foolishness unto him; neither can he know them.
[3]John 3:3, Except a man be born again, he cannot see the kingdom of God. John 3:5;1:12; Hebrews 12:14, And holiness, without which no man shall see the Lord. Colossians 1:14; Titus 3:5.

1. HIS TITLES. The Bible ascribes to Christ the titles of Saviour[1], Jehovah[2], Lord of hosts[3], the first and the last[4], God[5], true God[6], great God[7], God over all[8], mighty God, and the everlasting Father[9].

[1]Isaiah 45:21, There is no God else beside me; a just God and a Saviour; there is none beside me. Isaiah 43:10, 11, Beside me there is no Saviour. John 4:42,
This is indeed the Christ, the Saviour of the world.
Philippians 3:20;2 Timothy 1: 10; Titus 2:13.
[2]Psalm 83: 18, Whose name alone is JEHOVAH. Isaiah 40:3, The voice of him that crieth in the wilderness. Prepare ye the way of the Lord (Jehovah). Luke 1:76.
[3]Isaiah 8:13, 14, Sanctify the LORD of hosts himself; and let him be your fear, and let him be your dread. And he shall be for a sanctuary; but for a stone of stumbling and for a rock of offense to both the houses of Israel. 1 Peter 2:4 6; Isaiah 6:5; John 12:41.
[4]Revelation 22: 13,1 am Alpha and Omega, the beginning and the end, the first and the last. Isaiah 44:6; Revelation 1: 1, 11.
[5]1Timothy 3:16, God was manifest in the flesh. 1 John 3:16; John 1:1, Hebrews 1:8; John 20:28, 29.
[6] 1 John 5:20, we are in him that is true, even in his Son Jesus Christ. This is the true God and eternal life.
[7] Titus 2:13, Looking for that blessed hope, and the glorious appearing of the great God, and our Saviour Jesus Christ.
[8] Romans 9:5, of whom as concerning the flesh Christ came, who is over all, God blessed for ever.
[9] Isaiah 9:6, For unto us a child is born, unto us a son is given; and the government shall be upon his shoulder; and his name shall be called Wonderful, Counselor, The Mighty God, The Everlasting Father, The Prince of Peace.

Other Studies: John 16:27; Matthew 1:18, 20; Luke 1:35; Mark 7:1; John 1:34; John 30:31; John3:16; John 1:18; John 16:13; I Corinthians 2:11; Genesis 1:2; Acts 8:39; 10:19; I Corinthians 2:13; Acts 21:11; John 14:26; Acts 13:2; Acts 16:6; Acts 13:4; John 16:8; Genesis 6:3; Mark 3:29; Isaiah 63:10; Acts 7:51; Ephesians 4:30; Hebrews 9:14; Psalm 139:7; I Corinthians 2: 10; Nehemiah 9:20; Psalm 143:10; John 14:17; Job 33:4; Job 26:13; Psalm 104:30; 2 Peter 2:21; I Peter 3:18; Romans 8:11; I Corinthians 6:11.

The Holy Spirit

1. The Scriptures ascribe to the Holy Spirit the acts and attributes of an intelligent Being. He is said to guide[2], to know[3], to move[4], to give information[5], to comrnand[6], to forbid[7], to send forth[8], to reprove.
2. The attributes of God are ascribed to the Holy Spirit; such as eternity[2], Omnipotent[3], Omniscience[4], Goodness[5], and Truth[6].
3. The works of God are ascribed to the Holy Spirit; creation[2], inspiration[3], giving of life[4], and sanctification[5].
4. The same acts which in one part of the Bible are attributed to the Holy Spirit are in other parts said to be performed by God.
5. The apostles assert that the Holy Spirit is Lord and God. From the foregoing the conclusion is that the Holy Spirit is in reality God, and one with the Father in all divine perfections. It has also been shown that Jesus Christ is God—one with the Father. Then these three, the Father, the Son, and the Holy Ghost are united in the authority by which believers are baptized, and in the benedictions pronounced by the

21

Apostles, which are acts of the highest-religious worship.

[1]Isaiah 6:8, 9, I heard the voice of the Lord, And He said, Go, and tell this people. Hear ye, indeed, but understanding not. Acts 28:25, 26, Well spake the Holy Ghost. Go unto this people, and say, Hearing ye shall hear, and shall not understand.
[2] 2 Corinthians 3: 17, Now the Lord is that Spirit. Acts 5:3, 4, Why hath Satan filled thine heart to lie to the Holy Ghost...Thou hast not lied unto men, but unto God.
[3] Matthew 28:19, Go ye, therefore, and teach all nations, baptizing them in the name of the Father, and of the Son, and of the Holy Ghost. 2 Corinthians 13:14, The grace of the Lord Jesus Christ, and the love of God, and the communion of the Holy Ghost, be with you all. I Peter 1:2.

The Incarnation of Christ

The Word, which in the beginning was with God and which was God, by whom all things were made, condescended to a state of humiliation in being united with human nature and becoming like us, pollution and is excepted[1] in this state, as a subject of the law, he was liable to the infirmities of our nature[2]; was tempted as we are[3]; but lived our example[4] and rendered perfect obedience to the divine requirements[5]. As Christ was made of the seed of David according to the flesh, he is called "the Son of Man" [6], and as the divine existence is the fountain from which he proceeded, and was the only agency by which he was begotten.

22

1. **THE ATONEMENT.** As sin cannot be pardoned without a sacrifice, and the blood of beasts could never wash away sin, Christ gave Himself a sacrifice for the sins of the world[7], and thus made salvation possible for all men[8]. He died for us, suffering in our stead, to make known the righteousness of God, that He might be just in justifying sinners who believe in His Son'.

[1]John 1: 14, And the Word was made flesh and dwelt among us. Philippians 2:6, 7, Who, being in the form of God, thought it not robbery to be equal with God; but made himself of no reputation, and took upon him the form of a servant, and was made in the likeness of men. 2 Corinthians 8:9; Hebrews 4:15.

[2] Hebrews 2:17, Wherefore, in all things, it behooved him to be made like unto his brethren. Matthew 8:17; 5:2; 8:24; John 11:33, 35; 19:28; Isaiah 55:3; Luke 22:44.

[3] Hebrews 4: 15, Was in all points tempted like as we are. Matthew 4: 1-11.

[4]1 Peter 2:21, Leaving us an example, that ye should follow his steps. John 13:15; I John 2:6. [5]Isaiah 42:21, He will magnify the law, and make it honorable. Matthew 5:17; 3:15; Galatians 4:4. [6]Luke 19: 10, For the Son of man is come to seek and to save that which was lost.

[7]1 John 2:2, And he is the propitiation for our sins; and not for ours only, but also for the sins of the whole world. Isaiah 53:5; 10:11; Romans 4:25; Matthew 20:28; I Peter 3:18; John 1:29; Hebrews 9:26; Romans 5:6, 8.

[8]Titus 2:11, For the grace of God that bringeth salvation has appeared to all men. Hebrews 2:9, That he by the grace of God should taste death for every man. I Timothy 2:6; Isaiah

45:22; Peter 3:9; 2 Corinthians 5: 14, 15; I Timothy 4:10.

Through the redemption effected by Christ, salvation is actually enjoyed in the world, and will be enjoyed in the next by all who do not in this life refuse obedience to the known requirements of God[7]. The atonement of sin was necessary[3], for present and future, obedience can no more blot our past sins than past obedience can remove the guilt of present and future sins. Had God pardoned the sins of men without satisfaction for the violations of his law, it would follow that transgression might go on with impunity, government would be abrogated, and the obligation of obedience to God would be in effect, removed.

    2. **MEDIATION OF CHRIST.** Our Lord not only died for our sins, but He arose for our justification[4]; and ascended to heavens where, as Mediator between God and man, He will make intercession for men till the final judgment.

The Gospel Call

The call of the Gospel is coextensive with the atonement to all men[6]. Both by the world and the strivings of the Spirit[1]; so that salvation is rendered equally possible to all[2]; and, if any fail of eternal life, the fault is wholly their own[3].

[1]Romans 3:25, 26, When God hath set forth to be a propitiation, through faith in his blood, to declare his righteousness for the remission of sins that are past, through the forbearance of God; to declare, I say, at this time his righteousness; that he might be just, and the justifier of

24

which believeth in Jesus. Romans 5:9, 18; Matthew 26:28; Ephesians 1 :7; Revelation 5:9; I Peter 2:24.

[2]Romans 5:18, Therefore, as by the offense of one judgment came upon all men of condemnation to them which are in Christ Jesus, who walk not after the flesh, but after the spirit. Mark 16:15; Romans 2:14, 15.

[3] Hebrews 9:22, Without shedding of blood is no remission. Ephesians 1:7, In whom we have redemption through his blood, the forgiveness of sins. Romans 5:19.

[4] Romans 4:25, Who was delivered for our offenses, and was raised again for our justification. I Corinthians 15:17.

[5] Acts 1:11, This same Jesus, which is taken up from you into heaven. Mark 16:19.

[6] Mark 16:15, Go ye into all the world, and preach the gospel to every creature. Isaiah 45:22, Look unto me, and be saved, all the ends of the earth. Proverbs 8:24; Isaiah 55: 1; Revelation 22:17.

Repentance

The repentance which the Gospel requires includes a deep conviction, a penitential sorrow, an open confession, a decided hatred and an entire forsaking of all sin[4]. This repentance God has enjoined on all men; and without it in this life the sinner must perish eternally[5].

Faith

Saving faith is an assent of the mind to the fundamental truths of Revelation 6, and acceptance of the Gospel, through the influence of the Holy Spirit[1] and a firm confidence and trust in Christ[2]. The fruit of faith is obedience to the Gospel[3]. The power to believe is the gift of God[4], but believing is an act of the creature, which is required as a condition of pardon, and without which the sinner cannot obtain salvation[5]. All men are required to believe in Christ, and those who yield obedience to this requirement become the children of God by faith[6].

[1]Joel 2:28, I will pour out my Spirit upon all flesh. John 16:8; John I :9; Isaiah 55:11; Luke 2:10.

[2]1 Timothy 2:4, Who will have all men to be saved, and come unto the knowledge of the truth. Acts 10:34, God is no respector of persons. Ezekiel 33:11; 2 Peter 3:9.

[3]Hosea 13:9, O Israel, thou hast destroyed thyself. Proverbs 1:24; Isaiah 65:12; Jeremiah 7:13,14; Zechariah 7:11,13; John 5:40, And ye will not come to me, that ye might have life. Matthew 23:37.

[4]2 Corinthians 7: 10, For godly sorrow worketh repentance to salvation not to be repented of. Psalm 51:17; Proverbs 28:13, He that covereth his sins shall not prosper; but who so confesseth and forsaketh them, shall have mercy. Psalm 32:5; Ezekiel 36:31, then shall ye remember your own evil ways, and your doings that were not good, and shall loathe yourselves in your own sight for your iniquities and for your abominations. Psalm 51:3, 4; Ezekiel 18:30, Repent, and turn yourselves from all your transgressions; so iniquity shall not be your ruin.

[5]Acts 17:30, But not commandeth all men everywhere to repent. Luke 13:15, But except ye repent, ye shall all likewise perish. Acts 3:19.

[6]Hebrews 11:6, He that cometh to God must believe that he is, and that he is a rewarder of them that diligently seek him. Hebrews 11:1, Faith is the substance of things hoped for, the evidence of things not seen. John 5:46, 47; Romans 10:9.

As man is a fallen and sinful being, he must be regenerated, in order to obtain salvation[7]. This change is an instantaneous renewal of the heart by the Holy Spirit[8], whereby the penitent sinner receives new life, becomes a child of God[9], and is disposed to serve Him[10]. This is called in Scripture being born again—born of the Spirit[1], being quickened[2] passing from death unto life[3], and a partaking of the divine nature[4].

[1]Romans 10:10, With the heart man believeth unto righteousness. Galatians 5:22, But the fruit of the Spirit is...faith. I Corinthians 13:8, 9.
[2]Acts 16:31. Believe on the Lord Jesus Christ, and thou shalt be saved. John 3:16; Romans 4:20-22; Ephesians 3:12.
[3]James 2: 17, Faith, if it hath not works, is dead, being alone. Galatians 5:6, I Timothy 1:5.
[4]Philippians I :29, unto you it is given in the behalf of Christ. . .to believe on him.2 Peter 1:1; Ephesians 2:8.
[5]John 3:36, He that believeth on the Son hath everlasting life; and he that believeth not the Son shall not see life; but the wrath of God abideth on him. Mark 16: 16, John 8:21, 24; Hebrews 11:6.
[6]John 1:7, That all men through him might believe. Galatians 3:26, Ye are all the children of God by faith in Christ Jesus. Acts 10:43; Romans 5: 1; John 3:15.
[7]John 3:3, Except a man be born again, he cannot see the kingdom of God. Hebrews 12:13; Revelation 21:27; Galatians 5:19-21.
[8]John 3:5, Except a man be born...of the Spirit, he cannot enter into the kingdom of God. John 1:13; Ezekiel 36:26, 27;Titus 3:5; Ephesians 2:10.
[9]Romans 8:16, The Spirit itself beareth witness with our

spirit, that we are the children of God. John 1:12; 5:25, James 1: 18, 2 Corinthians 5:17.

[10]Ezekiel 11:19, 20, And I will give them one heart, and I will put a new spirit within you; and I will take the stony heart out of their flesh, and will give them a heart of flesh; that they may walk in my statutes, and keep mine ordinances, and do them. I Peter 2:5.

Justification and Sanctification

1. **JUSTIFICATION.** Personal justification implies that the person justified has been guilty before God; and, in consideration of the atonement of Christ, accepted by faith, the sinner is pardoned and absolved from the guilt of sin and restored to the divine favor[5]. Christ's atonement is the foundation of the sinner's redemption, yet, without repentance and faith, it can never give him justification and peace with God[6].

2. **SANCTIFICATION** is the continuing of God's grace by which the Christian may constantly grow in grace and in the knowledge of our Lord Jesus Christ[7].

Perseverance of the Saints

There are strong grounds to hope that the truly regenerate will persevere unto the end, and be saved, through the power of divine grace which is pledged for their support[1]; but their future obedience and final salvation are neither determined nor certain, since through infirmity and manifold temptations they are in danger of falling; and they ought

28

therefore to watch and pray, lest they make shipwreck of their faith and be lost[2].

[1]John 3:6, That which is born of the Spirit is spirit. John 3:5-8; 1 John 4:7; 5:1.
[2]Ephesians 2: 1, You hath he quickened. who were dead in trespasses and sins. Psalm 119:50, 93; Ephesians 2:5; Colossians 2: 13.
[3]John 5:24, He that heareth my word, and believeth on him that sent me...is passed from
death unto life. I John 3:14.
[4]2 Peter 1:4, That by these ye might be partakers of the divine nature. Hebrews 3:14.
[5]Romans 5: 1, Therefore, being justified by faith, we have peace with God
through our Lord Jesus Christ. Romans 5: 16, The free gift is of many offenses unto justification. Acts 13:39; Isaiah 53:11.
[6]Acts 3:19, Repent ye, therefore, and be converted, that your sins may be blotted out. Hebrews 4:2; 11:6; Romans 9:31, 32; Acts 13:38, 39.
[7]1 Thessalonians 5:23, And the very God of peace sanctify you wholly; and I pray God that your whole spirit and soul and body be preserved blameless unto the coming of our Lord Jesus Christ. 2 Corinthians 7: 1; 2 Peter 3:18, Grow in grace, and in the knowledge of our Lord and Saviour, Jesus Christ. Hebrews 6:1; I John 5:4; Colossians 4:12, Proverbs 4: 18; I John 1:7, 9; I
Peter 1:16.

The Sabbath

This is one day in seven, which from the creation of the world God has set apart for sacred rest and holy service[3].

Under the former dispensation, the seventh day of the week as commemorative of the work of the creation, was set apart for the Sabbath[4]. Under the Gospel, the first day of the week, in commemoration of the Resurrection of Christ, and by authority of Christ and the apostles, is observed as the Christian Sabbath[1]. On this day all men are required to refrain from secular labor and devote themselves to the worship and service of God[2].

[1]Romans 8:38,39, For I am persuaded, that neither death, nor life, nor angels, nor principalities, or powers, nor things present, nor things to come, nor height, nor depth, nor any other creature, shall be able to separate us from the love of God, which is in Christ Jesus our Lord. I Corinthians 10:13, God is faithful, who will not suffer you to be tempted above that ye are able; but will with the temptation also make a way to escape, that ye may be able to bear it. 2 Corinthians 12:9. My grace is sufficient for thee. Job 17:9; Matthew 16:18; John 10:27, 28; Philippians 1:6.

[2]2 Chronicles 15:2,The Lord is with you, while ye be with him...but if ye forsake him, he will forsake you. 2 Peter 1:10, Wherefore the rather, brethren, give diligence to make your calling and election sure; for if you do these things, ye shall never fall. Ezekiel 33:18, When the righteous turneth from his righteousness, and committeth iniquity, he shall even die there by. John 15:6; I Corinthians 10:12; Hebrews 6:4 6; 12:15; 1 Chronicles 28:9; Revelation 2:4; 1 Timothy 1:19; 2 Peter 2: 20, 21; 1 Corinthians 9:27; Matthew 24:13; Acts I:25; Revelation 22:19.

[3]Genesis 2:3, God blessed the seventh day, and sanctified it. Mark 2:27, The sabbath was made for man. Nehemiah 9:14.

[4]Exodus 20:8-11, Remember the sabbath day, to keep it holy. six days shalt thou labor, and do all thy work; but the

seventh day is the sabbath of the Lord thy God; in it thou shalt not do any work, thou, nor thy son, nor thy daughter, thy manservant, nor thy maidservant, nor thy cattle, nor thy stranger that is within thy gates. For in six days the Lord made heaven and earth, the sea, and all that in them is, and rested the seventh day; wherefore the Lord blessed the Sabbath day, and hallowed it.

The Church

A CHRISTIAN CHURCH is an organized body of believers in Christ, who statedly assemble to worship God, and who sustain the ordinances of the Gospel agreeably to His Word[3]. In a more general sense, it is the whole body of Christians throughout the world, and none but the regenerate is its real members[4]. Believers are admitted to a particular church on their giving evidence of faith, being baptized, and receiving the hand of fellowship[5].

[1]Luke 24: 1-7, Now upon the first day of the week, very early in the morning, they came unto the sepulcher...He is not here, but is risen. Luke 24:33-36; John 20:19, 26; Acts 2:1; 20:7, And upon the first day of the week, when the disciples came together to break bread, Paul preached unto them. I Corinthians 16:2; Revelation I: 10; Psalm 118:23-24.
[2]Isaiah 58:13,14. If thou turn away thy foot from the sabbath, from doing thy pleasure on my holy day; and call the sabbath a delight, the holy of the Lord, honorable; and shall honor him, not doing thine own ways, nor finding thine own pleasure, nor speaking thine own words; then shalt thou delight thyself in the Lord. Isaiah 56:2; Exodus 20:8-11.
[3]1Corinthians 1:2, Unto the church of God which is at Corinth, to them that are sanctified in Christ Jesus, called to

be saints. Acts 2:41, 47; 20:7; I Corinthians 16:1, 2; Revelation 1:4.

[4]Ephesians 5:25, 27, Christ also loved the church and gave himself for it...That he might present it to himself a glorious church. Ephesians 1:22, 23; I Corinthians 12:27, 28; Colossians 1:18, 24; I Peter 2:5; John 18:36; John 15:2, 6.

[5]Acts 2:41, Then they that gladly received his word were baptized; and the same day there were added unto them about three thousand souls. Acts 8:12; Galatians 3:27.

The Gospel Ministry

1. **QUALIFICATION OF MINISTERS.** They must possess good, natural and acquired abilities[1] deep and ardent piety[2], be especially called of God to the work[3], and ordained by prayer and the laying on of hands[4].
2. **DUTIES OF MINISTERS.** These are to preach the Word[5], administer the ordinances of the Gospel[6], visit their people, and otherwise perform the work of faithful ministers[7].

Ordinances of the Gospel

1. **CHRISTIAN BAPTISM.** This is the immersion of believers in water, in the name of the Father, the Son, and the Holy Spirit[8], in which are represented the burial and Resurrection of Christ, the death of Christians to the world, the washing of their souls from the pollution of sin, their rising to newness of life, their engagement to serve God, and their resurrection at the last day[1].

[1]2 Timothy 2:15, Study to shew thyself approved unto God, a workman that needeth not to be ashamed, rightly dividing the word of truth. I Timothy 4:13-16, Till I come give attendance to reading, to exhortation, to doctrine, Neglect not the gift that is in thee.. Meditate upon these things, give thyself wholly to them; that thy profiting may appear to all. Titus 1:9; 2:7, 8; 2 Timothy I :7; 2:2; I Timothy 3:2-7.

[2]Psalm 50: 16, But unto the wicked, God saith, What hast thou to do to declare my statutes, or that thou shouldest take my covenant in thy mouth? 2 Timothy 1:8-11, 14; 2:22; 35;Titus 1:5-9; I Corinthians2:12-16.

[3]Acts 20:28, Take heed therefore unto yourselves, and to all the flock...over which the Holy Ghost hath made you overseers. Hebrews 5:4; I Corinthians 9: 16; Acts 13:2.

[4]1 Timothy 4:14, With the laying on of the hands of the presbytery. 2 Timothy I :6; Acts 13:3.

[5]Mark 16: 15, Go ye into all the world, and preach the gospel to every creature. 2 Timothy 4:2; 2 Corinthians 4:5; Ezekiel 33:7.

[6]Matthew 28:19,Teach all nations, baptizing them. Luke 22:19,20,This do in remembrance of me. Acts 20:11; 27:35; I Corinthians 11:23-28; 10:16.

[7]Hebrews 13: 17, They watch for your souls as they that must give account. I Peter 5:2, Feed the flock of God which is among you, taking the oversight thereof. Acts 20:28; Jeremiah 3:13.

[8]Matthew 28: 19, Baptizing (Greek immersing) them in the name of the Father, and of the Son, and of the Holy Ghost. Colossians 2:12, Buried with him in baptism, wherein also ye are risen with him. Acts 16:32-34; 2:41.

2.**THE LORD'S SUPPER.** This is a commemoration of the death of Christ for our sins, in the use of bread, which He made the emblem of His broken body; and the cup, the emblem of His shed blood[2]; and by it the believer express his love for Christ, his faith and hope in him, and pledges His perpetual fidelity[3].

It is the privilege and duty of all who have spiritual union with Christ thus to commemorate His death; and no man has a right to forbid these tokens to the least of His disciples[4].

Death and the Intermediate State

   1. **DEATH.** As a result of sin, all mankind are subject to the death of the body[5].

[1]Romans 6:4, Therefore we are buried with him by baptism into death; that like as Christ was raised up from the dead by the glory of the Father, even so we also should walk in newness of life. Colossians 3:3; 2:12; Titus 3:5; Galatians 3:27; I Corinthians 15:29.
[2]1 Corinthians 11 :23-26, For I have received of the Lord that which also I delivered unto you. That the Lord Jesus, the same night in which he was betrayed, took bread; And when he had given thanks, he brake it, and said, Take, eat: this is my body, which is broken for you; this do in remembrance of me. After the same manner also he took the cup, when he was supped, saying This cup is the new testament in My blood; this do ye as oft as ye drink it, in remembrance of me. For as often as ye eat this bread, and drink this cup, ye do shew the Lord's death till he comes. Matthew 26:26 28; Luke 22: 19, 20.
[3]1 Corinthians 10:16, The cup of blessing which we bless, it is not the communion of the body of Christ? The bread which

34

we break, is it not the communion of the body of Christ? 1
Corinthians 10: 21; 11:27-29.

[4]1 Corinthians 10:17, For we being many are one bread, and
one body; for we are all partakers of that one bread.
Matthew 26:27, Drink ye all of it. Romans 14: 1,19; 1
Corinthians 12:12; Acts 2:42; 20:7.

[5]Romans 5: 12, As by one man sin entered into the world,
and death by sin; and so death passed upon all men, for that
all have sinned. Hebrews 9:27, it is appointed unto men
once to die. 1 Corinthians 15:22; Psalm 89:48; Ecclesiastes
8:8.

2. **THE INTERMEDIATE STATE.** The soul does not die
with the body; but immediately after death enters
into a conscious state of happiness or misery,
according to the moral character here possessed[1].

Second Coming of Christ

The Lord Jesus, who ascended on high, and sits at the right
hand of God, will come again, to close the Gospel
dispensation, glorify his saints, and judge the world[2].

The Resurrection

The Scriptures teach the resurrection of the bodies of all
men at the last day, each in its own order, they that have
done good will come forth to the resurrection of life, and they
that have done evil, to the resurrection of damnation[3].

1. **THE GENERAL JUDGMENT.** There will be a general judgment, when time and man's probation will close forever[1]. Then all men will be judged according to their works[2].

[1]Ecclesiastes 12:7, Then shall the dust return to the earth as it was; and the spirit shall return unto God who gave it. Philippians 1:23, Having a desire to depart, and to be with Christ which is far better. Luke 23:43; Matthew 17:2; 22:31,32; Acts 7:59; Matthew 10:28; 2 Corinthians 5:6; Luke 16:22-26; Revelation 6:9.
[2]Acts 1:11, This same Jesus which is taken up from you into heaven, shall so come in like manner as ye have seen him go into heaven. Matthew 25:31; I Corinthians 15:24, 28; I Thessalonians 4:15-17; 2 Thessalonians 1:7-10; 2 Peter 3:13; Matthew 24:42, 44.
[3]John 5:28, 29, The hour is coming, in which all that are in the graves shall hear his voice, and shall come forth; they that have done good, unto the resurrection of life; and they that have done evil, until the resurrection of damnation. Acts 24:15; 1 Corinthians 15:22, 23; 2 Timothy 2:18; Philippians 3:21; 1 Corinthians 15:35-55; Daniel 12:2.

2. **FUTURE RETRIBUTIONS.** Immediately after the general judgment, the righteous will enter into eternal life and the wicked will go into a state of endless punishments[3].

[1]Acts 17:31, Because he hath appointed a day, in which he will judge the world in righteousness. I Corinthians 15:24; Revelation 10:6; 22:11; 2 Peter 3:11, 12; Ecclesiastes 9:10.

[2] 2 Corinthians 5:10, For we must appear before the judgment seat of Christ; that every one may receive the things done in his body, according to that he hath done. whether it be good or bad. Ecclesiastes 12:14, For God shall bring every work into judgment, with every secret thing, whether it be good, or whether it be evil. Matthew 12:36; Revelation 20:12; Romans 2:16.

[3] Matthew 25:46, And these shall go away into everlasting punishment; but the righteous into life eternal.

2 Thessalonians 1:8-10. Taking vengeance on them that know not God, and that obey not the gospel of our Lord Jesus Christ; who shall be punished with everlasting destruction from the presence of the Lord, and from the glory of his power; when he shall come to be glorified in his saints. Romans 6:23; 2 Peter 1:11; Mark 3:29; 9:43, 44; Judges 7; Revelation 14:11; 21:2, 3, 4; Matthew 13:41-43; Romans 2:6-10.

I. The Marriage of Ministers

1. The Ministers of Christ are not commanded by God's Law either to vow the estate of single life, or to abstain from marriage; therefore, it is lawful for them, as for all other Christians, to marry at their own discretion, as they shall judge the same to serve better to godliness.

II. Divorce

2. Our Ministers shall discourage the procurement of divorce except on Scriptural grounds.

III. Temperance

3. The Holy Scriptures teach us to abstain from all alcoholic drinks. A large proportion of the crime and pauperism of this country is caused by strong drink. We do approve of all lawful and Christian efforts to exterminate the traffic and to save society from the evil results of intemperance.

Church Organization and Membership
The Order of a Church When Organized

The order of a church, when organized, shall be as follows:
1. There must be a duly approved, ordained United American Free Will Baptist minister as the Pastor.
2. She must be a member of the District Union, as assigned by the Annual Bishop .
3. There should be members enough to fill all the public offices in the church in order that a regular discipline may be kept.
4. On the day set apart for the acceptance of such Church, the members shall be examined by three Elders of our faith, and if they are found orthodox, the Bible is presented as the only rule of faith and practice.
   a) The church covenant is accepted.
   b) A prayer of consecration is offered.
   c) The hand of fellowship is given.
   d) A copy of the Book of Discipline shall be presented and the membership should be encouraged to become familiar with the Laws and Rules that govern our church.
   e) Then they shall become a body with all the rights common to that of any United American Free Will Baptist Church.

Joiner's Questionnaire

The pastor, or the presiding officer shall be expected to follow the procedures outlined below, for persons seeking membership in the local church.

1. Do you come forth to join this Church?
2. Do you believe that Jesus Christ is the Son of God and that He died for your sins?
3. It is the practice of the United American Free Will Baptist Denomination to baptize by immersion. Have you been baptized by immersion? If not, are you willing to be baptized by immersion?
4. Are you willing to abide by the laws, rules, and Discipline of the Church to the best of your knowledge?

If the above questions are answered satisfactorily, the minister, or person in authority may receive the candidate for membership.

After baptism, the right hand of fellowship may be given at the time selected by the pastor or person in authority. A special charge shall be given to the new member in regards to their duties and relationship to God, the church, and pastor. Immediately after a candidate is received for membership, the pastor shall initiate a plan of instruction to familiarize the member with the laws and procedures that govern the church.

Meetings of the Church

1. The Church of Jesus Christ being of the United American Free Will Baptist order, do covenant and agree, that four times a year, viz, every three months, to assemble for the purpose of holding a Godly Conference, the members being all present with convenience. Then and there the business of the Church shall be done. (Conferences may be held

more often, as the needs of the Church require.)

2. The conference is always to open and adjourn with praise and prayer to God.
3. During conference the members shall act, with all decency and good order.
4. But one shall speak at a time, and that by order, first addressing the Presiding Officer.
5. All matters shall be decided by a majority vote.
6. All quarterly conferences shall be held on any day of the week except on Sunday.
7. Every Church having a pastor shall commune and wash one another's feet every quarterly meeting.
8. Prayer and testimony meetings shall be held as often as may be thought proper, and should be encouraged by all members.
9. The officers of each Church shall hold a business meeting once a month. The pastor being the chairman ex officio.
10. The right of members to meet in the absence of the pastor shall not be denied. However, the pastor should be informed of all meetings which affect his own welfare or that of the church.
11. The General Bishop and Annual Bishop are empowered to intervene in a church dispute or conflict on the Annual level by the written request of either side of the conflict.

The Church Quarterly Conference

It is highly recommended that an agenda be used at all Quarterly Conferences.

Order of Business

1. Devotion
2. Official Roll and Qualification of Officers
3. Reading minutes, correct and approve.
4. Unfinished business.
5. New business.
6. Report of all the officers.
7. How many members sick and disabled?
8. What provisions have been made for widows and orphans?
9. Report on prayer meetings.
10. Report from all auxiliaries.
11. Call the member roll, collect dues (if applicable).
12. Financial Reports
13. Dismissal

Order of Worship

- Prelude
- Call to Worship
- Opening Hymn Invocation Choral Response Hymn
- Affirmation of Faith Scripture
- Prayer Hymn
- Benevolent Offering Church Announcements Inspiration Selection Sermon

- Invitation to the Unsaved
- Offering
- Benediction

(The offering may be taken before the sermon if the church chooses.)

- **Special Services**

Let each service consist of praise, the reading of Scripture, prayer, singing, preaching (if a worship service), offering, announcements, and doxology. It is recognized that each church must plan to suit its own needs in many situations.

Discipline and Government of the Church

1. No individual offense shall come before the Church Conference until the Gospel in the following words shall be complied with: Matthew 18:15,16, 17 verses. "Moreover if thy brother shall trespass against thee, go and tell him his fault between thee and him alone; if he shall hear thee, thou hast gained thy brother. But if he will not hear thee, then take with thee one or two more, that in the mouth of two or three witnesses every word may be established. And if he shall neglect to hear them, tell it unto the church; but if he neglect to hear the church, let him be unto thee as an heathen man and a publican."
2. If members shall walk disorderly and their offenses shall be public, then the Church shall be at liberty to publicly deal with them. Complaints must be lodged in time of conference, and if the accused be not present, they shall be cited to attend the following conference and they shall be dealt with as may be thought proper.
3. In case of a private nature, admonition and satisfaction shall be sufficient.

4. If members shall lay themselves liable to be dealt with, and the Church lodge a complaint against them, and cite them to attend the following conference; if they fail to attend, the Church not knowing the cause, the trial of the case may be postponed until the next conference and as long as the Church may think proper.

5. If any member shall walk in a disorderly manner from report only, if the report deserves notice, the Church shall investigate it and cite the member to attend a Board of Conference Meeting, and answer the complaint. If the complaint is owned out of the member's mouth, the church shall proceed as is thought proper. If the member denies the charge and sufficient evidence is not produced to show guilt, the case shall be dismissed.

6. If any member, by disorderly conduct, shall be liable to excommunication, no Church or pastor shall be at liberty, to expel the member, without the approval of the church. Yet, by the church, they may set aside from communion until satisfaction is given.

7. Any member found frequently at places of disorder, without lawful business, shall be censured by the Church, and said member shall make the Church satisfied or be dealt with as the Conference may think proper.

8. No testimony out of the church shall be taken against members in the Church, except in cases of disputes.

9. Every Church shall have a right to borrow money on its property for its own welfare, or connectional interest, by obtaining the approval of the Church Body.

10. No church of the U.A.F.W.B. Denomination shall be without a pastor more than ninety days if a regular Ordained Elder can be secured. When the members of a church for any reason fail to elect a Pastor after being without one for ninety days, the Annual Bishop shall send a pastor for the remainder of the Conference year. This shall be done with

the officers and members duly notified. When a church is without a pastor, the Annual Bishop shall supervise the religious administration of that church, until a regular ordained minister has been elected. The church shall make every possible effort to elect a pastor within ninety days.

11. No program or project of service shall be held in the Church without the pastor's approval. And if it is approved by the pastor, he shall encourage, and promote its welfare. The pastor must be careful not to be arbitrary or unchristian in any matter affecting the church.

12. All members shall attend public worship at their own church on the meeting days of their church, or be excused by their pastor. Officers, who fail to do this without lawful excuse, shall forfeit their right to office.

13. All members are tributaries to their respective churches and shall pay for the support of their pastor and other church expenses. For any delinquency a just reason must be given.

14. All members, in good standing according to the following rule, may vote in the church, and the majority vote shall be legal. However, in contested controversial or legal matters the voting age shall be 18 years of age.

A member is defined as one who willingly came forward under godly conviction and united with the local assembly (church). One who answered in the affirmative to the Joiner's Questionnaire as is recorded in the Book of Discipline and was accepted into the membership either by the approval of the church body or by the authority of the presiding pastor.

A member in good standing is interpreted as follows: The member MUST, as enabled by God:

- **ATTEND WORSHIP SERVICES**

Shall attend services regularly and participate in the activities of the church.

- **COMMUNE**

Shall partake of the Lord's Supper and the Washing of one another's feet as set forth in the Discipline of the U.A.F.W.B. Church and in keeping with (1 Corinthians 11:26; John 13:3-10; 12-17).

- **SUPPORT THE CHURCH FINANCIALLY**

Shall give regularly as taught in Malachi 3:8-12; Luke 6:38; 1 Corinthians 16:2; 2 Corinthians 9:7.

- **BE A WITNESS** (Matthew 5: 14; 16)
- **BE MISSIONARY MINDED**

Should be concerned with the winning of others to Christ. Proverbs 11:30.

- **BE AN EXAMPLE OF JESUS CHRIST**

(2 Corinthians 5:17)

The Member SHOULD, practice the Free Will Baptist Code of Ethics For Members as is found in the Book of Discipline.

15. Every deacon, who fails deliberately, to meet the duties and obligations that the law involves upon him, shall be removed from office.

16. Any deacon who uses a preacher to conduct services that has been silenced or expelled by the Annual Conference, shall be removed from his office, if he was previously notified by the conference authorities of the unqualified character of such minister.

17. If an officer or member of the church fail to work in harmony for the best interest of his church and the necessary labor to bring harmony fails with such an officer or member, he or she shall be removed from office, or may be expelled from the church by the Church and pastor.

18. No Church shall withdraw from her pastor before the conference year expires without first asking for his resignation ninety days in advance. Any church who does not comply with this regulation shall pay the pastor for three

months.

19. The pastor of a church shall have general oversight of his church. The officers and members shall be subject to the pastor's direction in accordance with the law.

20. Any church that has 50 members, the pastor should serve it at least two Sundays. With 300 or more members, the church should be a stationed church.

21. All Annual Conference, Convention and Union assessments, shall be appropriated by the church, and the same forwarded by the pastor or delegate for reporting.

22. The pastor who fails to work for the best interest of the church over which he presides, to keep peace and harmony among the members, or to encourage strict compliance with the requests, rules, and regulations of the Annual Conference, shall be subject to a charge and a trial before a Council of Triers.

23. No member of the church shall continue to hold a position who fails to perform the duties that the law requires of that position.

24. The Pastor and the Church shall be responsible to the Annual Conference for the payment of budgets assigned by the Annual and General Conference. For failure or violation, they shall be dealt with by the Annual Conference in accordance with the law.

25. There shall no indebtedness be brought against the church without the knowledge of the Church and pastor.

26. There shall be no church funds disbursed without the knowledge of the Church and pastor.

27. Every church shall have an election of all officers, annually, in the month of July. The election of the pastor shall be in accordance with the following rule of the United American Free Will Baptist Church:

28. "Once a pastor is elected to serve a church, they shall remain as pastor until either they resign or they are asked to

resign by the church. In either case, a 90 day notice of intent must be given.

29. If the church wants the immediate vacancy of the pulpit, it shall be the obligation of the church to compensate the pastor for 90 days. If the pastor chooses to leave the church immediately then he must compensate the church for 90 days."

Procedure:
If a pastor chooses to resign his pastorate, it is his duty to officially notify the church in writing.

If a church is going to request the resignation of the pastor, it is incumbent upon the church to set a date, giving proper notice to those members who are in good standing of the purpose and requesting them to come and vote. The majority rule in this matter shall stand. The pastor must be notified of the church's decision in writing.

Duties of Officers

"Every person holding an office in the church should be a born-again Christian."

Recording Secretary

It shall be the duty of the Recording Secretary to keep a true record of the business of the church in a book procured for that purpose and make a report of same at the Quarterly Conference.

Financial Secretary

It shall be the duty of the Financial Survey to keep an accurate record of all money received into the church through all means and from all sources. After receiving and recording the same, shall forward monies to the Church Treasurer for deposit.
The Financial Secretary shall be subject to the church or official board when requested.
The Financial Secretary shall sign all church checks and shall maintain a true record of all checks issued.

Treasurer

Every Church Treasurer shall be entrusted with all the funds of the Church. Shall keep a true account of all monies and other valuables received, and from whom, and make a report of the same to the Church. The treasurer shall sign all Church checks issued. The Treasurer shall be subject to the direction of the Trustees from time to time and his accounts shall be subject to the inspection of the pastor.

Mothers

Every Church shall elect Mothers according to the needs of the Church, who shall make the necessary preparation for the Lord's Supper. It shall be their duty to settle delicate cases between sisters and to instruct the young women in the way of the Lord.

Mothers shall be expected to follow the rules that are outlined in the *Free Will Baptist Deacons and Mothers Handbook.*

Pastor's Steward

There shall be a Pastor's Steward appointed in each Church to serve for one year. They shall be subject to reappointment by the pastor. It shall be their duty to see that all necessary provisions are made for the temporal comfort of the pastor in charge, and they shall constitute members of the regular Board of the Church. They shall be subject to the Quarterly Conference. Any delinquency on the part of the Pastor's Steward will be sufficient for removal from office.

Sexton

A Sexton shall be appointed by the Official Board in each

Church. It shall be the duty of the Sexton to open up the church on time, to keep it in decent order for Divine Worship services, to care for the grounds, to recommend necessary improvements to the Board. He should be adequately compensated, according to the ability of the Church.

Deacons

Deacons are elected annually consisting of not less than two nor more than seven members, according to the particular need of each church. It is their duty to serve its needy members, to visit the sick, to assist the pastor in promoting order and attendance upon the means of grace, to see that an efficient Scriptural discipline be enforced in the Church and to conduct religious meetings in the absence of the pastor. All to be done at the expense of the Church. The deacons must be by the Church considered spiritual men, holding the mystery of the faith in a pure conscience, ruling well in their own home (I Timothy 3:8-13).
After the deacons are elected by order of the church conference (before they act officially), the pastor shall set apart a time of prayer and fasting for the purpose of their ordination, and call on such help as he may think proper and qualify them for all the designed purposes of their appointment. They shall also be expected to follow the rules that are outlined in the Free Will Baptist Deacons and Mothers Handbook.

Ruling Elders

Every Church shall elect annually, a Board of Ruling Elders according to the needs of the Church. The business of the

Ruling Elders, after their qualification, shall be to settle controversies between the members. It shall be legal for them to take such testimony, both in and out of the Church, as shall enable them to pass a true and right judgment, with the approval of the pastor.

When the Ruling Elders have full information of any matter respecting controversies between the members, should they find a fraud intended, they shall be at liberty to give the injured party right to common law, and make a report thereof to the next Quarterly Conference at which time the offending party may be set aside from communion until the controversy is settled.

If any member shall fly from judgment of the Ruling Elders it shall be open excommunication, and the pastor shall make known such excommunication by the declaration of the same before the Church. (This means the person is no longer a member of the Church.)

Trustee Board and How It's Constituted

1. Every Church shall elect a Trustee Board, which shall not consist of not less than three persons.
2. Each member of the Trustee Board shall not be less than twenty-one years of age, and members in good standing in the United American Free Will Baptist Church.
3. Where there is no specific requirement of the common law they shall be elected annually by the church.
4. The Board of Trustees of every Church shall be responsible to the Quarterly Conference of said Church; and shall be required to present a written report of its acts at every Quarterly Conference.

5. No Trustee shall be rejected while he is in joint security for money unless such relief be given him by the Board and pastor.
6. It shall be the duty of the Board of Trustees to take charge and protect the Church property, with all its appurtenances, in trust for the membership, and to make such improvements as may be necessary from time to time for the interest of the Society of which they are Trustees; and to see that order and decorum are at all times observed in the Church.
7. The Pastor is ex officio Chairman of the Board of Trustees.

Members

The Free Will Baptist Code of Ethics for Members

1. Never speak ill or disparagingly of your pastor.
2. If what you are about to say is not for the good of all concerned, don't say it.
3. It is the duty of members to be just, courteous, and Christian in all their relationships with the pastor and other members.
4. Members should not speak disparagingly of one another, but, rather, watch over each other in brotherly love.
5. Every member should practice the principles of the Christian religion.
6. Every home should subscribe to the church paper, and have a "Book of Discipline" in order that all members will be well informed.
7. It is the duty of members to assume all the duties and

responsibilities of church membership according to our "Book of Discipline."

8. It is the duty of all members to attend and support every auxiliary of the church.

9. The confidential statements of the minister to officers, or members are privileged and should never be divulged without the consent of the minister making it.

10. If you are dissatisfied about something, talk it over privately with the pastor.

11. Before bringing controversial matters before the church, discuss it with the pastor.

12. Do not try to be the pastor. There are many ways to help the pastor.

13. Be honest, truthful, courteous, thoughtful, kind, and friendly.

14. Be Christian always, everywhere, in everything. Abound in good works.

The Ministry

The Minister and the Pastor

1. Every minister shall pay his annual conference assessments, unless he is lawfully excused by his annual conference. If he fails to satisfy his annual conference, he can be expelled from the annual conference.
2. All ministers shall be members of a district union, all annual conventions and the annual conference by virtue of office. He shall pay membership dues in each.
3. At the close of each annual conference, all licensed preachers and ordained ministers, entitled to, shall receive a Ministerial Certificate of Approval.
4. No minister shall fill any pastor's charge for the purpose of transacting any business other than preaching, without first consulting and conferring with the pastor in charge.
5. Every minister of this connection has a right to constitute branches of the same with permission from the annual or general bishop.
6. Every minister shall pay annual assessments as are imposed by the general church.
7. An ordained minister who pastors in more than one annual conference shall pay each annual conference dues that are imposed by the general church. Failing to pay in any conference forfeits his right to pastor in the bounds of the general church.
8. Every pastor of a church in the U.A.F.W.B. Denomination shall be responsible for the budgets,

fees and assessments for the district union, annual conventions and annual conference. These finances should be ready at the time and setting of each session and remittance of the same to its proper source should be prompt.

9. The pastor of the church should be notified of the sick, and the condition of the aged. He should encourage the members to help the needy. In cases, where the Pastor is needed or visitation is desired, a request should be made for the same. He shall stay informed as to sources and agencies offering help, aid, or assistance to these members in order that they might receive all available benefits intended for them.

10. Every church pastor shall be chosen out of the number of regular ministers, having a valid Ordination Certificate, and shall come into office by choice of the church.

11. The office of a pastor is to serve the church to which he is chosen in the administration of all the gospel ordinances and decrees of the church. He is to have the oversight and care of the ministry in the church over which he presides and may call to his assistance such persons as he may see fit.

12. The pastor shall have the right to reprimand any member under his care at any time. He shall have the right to cite any member to the next quarterly conference when the offense is committed between conferences.

13. No pastor shall withdraw from his charge or charges before his conference year expires without first tendering his resignation three months before maturity. Any pastor who does not comply with this regulation shall pay to the church of which he pastors his salary for three months. The church shall also

comply with this rule.

14. A minister, for transgression, shall be dealt with by his membership church or by any church over which he presides as pastor. It shall be the duty of the church to file a charge or complaint with the annual bishop. The bishop shall call three or five ministers who shall constitute a council and try the offender. If the transgressor renders satisfaction, the council may restore him to fellowship and office; but if sufficient satisfaction is not given, the council shall silence the offender. This council shall have power to acquit or silence the offender for a period of from one to twelve months.

Ministers From Other Churches

All ministers wishing to unite with us from any other church or denomination must prove that he is in good standing in his own church, before and at the time of his withdrawal there from, and must be, as far as we can determine, blameless in life and character.

No minister, coming from any other church or denomination to the U.A.F.W.B. Denomination for membership, shall be allowed to pastor any church or churches until they have held membership in the U.A.F.W.B. Denomination for a period of not less than twelve months, and receives a Ministerial Certificate of Approval from the Annual Conference of which they are a member.

After a minister has become a member of an annual conference, the bishop may transfer him to any other conference in the connection with his consent.

Ministers Code of Ethics

I. The Minister and His Work

1. No minister should seek in any way to obtain a church held by another minister.
2. Ministers should insist upon a salary scale commensurate with the demands laid upon him by the church and society.
3. Every pastor should recognize and perform all the duties of a pastor to the best of his ability.
4. It is the duty of the minister to maintain his own efficiency by study, by travel, and other means.
5. The minister should not try to use pressure to secure a position, a church, or any other favors.
6. It is unethical to fail to report to the duly constituted authority of the church any matters which are clearly detrimental to the welfare of the   church.
7. Ministers should never charge a fee for officiating at a funeral.
8. As a minister controls his own time he should make it a point of honor to give full service to his parish (church).
9. Part of the minister's service as a leader of his people is to reserve sufficient time for serious study in order to thoroughly understand his message, keep abreast

of current thought, and develop his intellectual and spiritual capacities.

10. It is equally the minister's duty to keep physically fit. A weekly holiday and an annual vacation should be taken and used for rest and improvement.

11. As a public interpreter of divine revelation and human duty, the minister should tell the truth as he sees it and present it tactfully and constructively.

12. As a spiritual leader in the community the minister must be honest, avoids debts, and meet his bills promptly.

13. The minister should be careful not to bring reproach on his calling by joining in marriage improper persons.

II. The Minister's Relations With His Church

1. It is unethical for a minister to break his contract made with the church.

2. As a professional man, the minister should make his service primary and the remuneration (salary) secondary. His training and efficiency, however, demands that he should receive a salary adequate to the work he is expected to do and in accordance with the scale of living in the church which he serves.

3. It is unethical for the minister to engage in other lines of remunerative work without the knowledge and consent of the church which he serves, or its official board.

4. The confidential statements made to a minister by his members are privileged and should never be divulged without the consent of those making them.

5. It is unethical for a minister to take sides with factions in his church.

6. The minister recognizes himself to be the servant of the community in which he resides or serves. Fees which are offered should be accepted only in the light of this principle.
7. I will dedicate my time and energy to the church which I serve, and to the Christian ministry and will maintain strict standards and discipline.

III. The Minister's Personal Conduct

1. The minister should cultivate his devotional life, continuing steadfastly in reading the Bible, meditation and prayer.
2. The minister should be fair to his family and endeavor to give them the time and consideration to which they are entitled.
3. The minister should try to live within his income and not leave carelessly unpaid debts behind him.
4. The minister should strive to grow in his work through comprehensive reading, careful study, attending the district unions, conventions, and annual conferences.
5. The minister should lead his congregation in giving and be honest in the stewardship of money.
6. The minister should not plagiarize. (Steal and pass on as one's own the ideas, writings, etc., of another.)
7. The minister should seek to be Christlike in his personal attitudes and conduct toward all people regardless of race, class or creed.

IV. The Minister's Relationship to Fellow Ministers

1. The minister should refuse to enter into unfair competition with other ministers in order to secure a

pulpit or place of honor.

2. The minister should seek to serve his fellow ministers and their families in every way possible and in no instance should he accept fees for such services.
3. The minister should never speak ill or disparagingly about the work of his predecessor or his successor.
4. The minister should refrain from frequent visits to a former field and if, in exceptional cases, he is called back for a funeral or a wedding, he should request that the resident minister be invited to participate in the service.
5. The minister should be courteous to fellow ministers at all times and especially kind and thoughtful of retired ministers.
6. I will not gossip about other ministers.
7. I will hold in sincere respect any minister whose work is well done, regardless of the size or the nature of the field he serves.
8. I will consider all ministers my co-laborers in the work of Christ, even though I may differ from them, I shall respect their Christian earnestness and sincerity.
9. I will never be guilty of proselytizing. (Trying to persuade one to leave his church to become a member of mine.)

V. The Minister's Relationship to His Community

1. I will strive to be human in all my relationships to the community but will never lower my standards in order to appear "A Good Fellow."
2. I will not be a party to a funeral or marriage racket.
3. I will be considerate of the working hours of business and professional men and will not consume their time with unimportant matters.

4. I consider that my first duty to my community is to be a conscientious pastor and leader of my own congregation, but will not use this fact as an excuse to escape reasonable responsibilities that the community calls upon me to assume.

VI. My Relationship to the Church Universal

1. I will give attention, sympathy, and when possible, support to the ecumenical church, recognizing that my church is a part of the church universal. I will not be slack in my efforts to help the church extend the Kingdom of God.

The Process of Trials

There shall be four levels at which all parishioners and administrators may have charges, complaints, or transgressions heard.

Office of the Presiding Minister

1.   The first step shall be the office of the presiding minister; parishioners, church members and church officers shall have all charges or complaints heard by the presiding minister of that church.

Council of Triers

2.   If there is an appeal by the parishioner or the church officer from the ruling of the presiding minister, then this appeal will be heard by a Council of Triers. The Council of Triers will be an appellate tribunal to hear all appeals from the presiding minister by parishioners and all officers of the church.

The Council of Triers will further be a tribunal of first instance for all presiding ministers. All charges, complaints or allegations of transgressions against presiding minister will first be heard by the Council of Triers. When a charge for transgression is made, it is the duty of the Annual Bishop to call three ministers who shall constitute a Council of Triers and try the offender. If the offender renders satisfaction, the Council may restore him to fellowship and office; but if sufficient satisfaction is not given, the Council shall silence the offender. This Council shall have power to acquit or silence the offender for a period of from one to twelve months. In case of an appeal, the case will be heard within thirty days by a Council of Appeals, appointed by the Bishop. This Council shall consist of five members who shall be a standing Council for twelve months. This Council has the right to silence an offender from one to twelve months or acquit.

Council of Intermediate Appeals

3.   If there is an appeal from the Council of Triers the same will be heard by a Council of Intermediate Appeals. The council of Intermediate Appeals will consist of five members of both clergy and lay members as appointed by the General Bishop. The members of the Council of Intermediate Appeals will hold office for a twelve month period. All appeals coming from the Council of Triers shall be heard by the Council of Intermediate Appeals within 30 days after the appeal has been granted by the Annual Bishop. This Council shall have the authority to reverse totally or partially; or approve any verdict of a lower council.

Council of Final Appeals

4.   If an appeal is taken against the verdict of the Council of Intermediate Appeals, by either the Council of Triers or the offender, the grounds for the appeal must be made in writing to the General Bishop within 10 days following the decision of the Council of Intermediate Appeals.
The General Bishop has the right to deny or allow the appeal. If granted, the General Bishop will appoint a

committee who shall be called Council of Final Appeals. They shall constitute a Council of Appeals for churches, ministers, officers, and all other causes that may have been found guilty by the decision of the Council of Intermediate Appeals. The decision of the Council of Final Appeals is final. This committee shall be appointed by the General Bishop and shall be approved by the General Conference and shall become a standing committee. When the General conference is not in session, any replacements to this committee shall be made by the General Bishop. This Council shall have the authority to reverse totally or partially, or approve any verdict of a lower council.

The District Union Meeting

PURPOSE:
The purpose of the District Union is to unite into a Christian Fellow ship those assigned churches in the district on each fifth weekend.
It is through this fellowship that the brotherhood is strengthened, that an exchange of ideas is shared and certain programs and information of the Annual Conference is channeled into the local churches.

1. The District Elder shall be appointed by the Annual Bishop and shall be paid such compensation as the Union Board may direct. He shall appoint an assistant, subject to the approval of the Annual Bishop.
2. The District Elder, Assistant District Elder, secretary and treasurer shall be standing officers, and shall be paid such compensation as the Union Board directs.
3. The District Elder shall deal with ministerial applicants according to our Book of Discipline.

The District Elder

This District Elder is an ordained minister appointed by the Annual Bishop to serve as the bishop's assistant in directing, interpreting and implementing the programs and directives of the Annual Conference. He is chief elder, responsible to the churches assigned to the district.

The District Elder is under the direct supervision of the Annual Bishop and will serve as chairman of committees appointed to do initial investigations of violations of law reported on the district as directed by the Annual Bishop. An exception to the chairmanship can be made at the discretion of the Annual Bishop.

Rules and Responsibilities

DEVELOPMENT
Assists assignees, directors or persons appointed on a district level by the General Church, General Departments or Annual Conference in implementing special assignments and programs.

MONITORING
Monitors matters that might impact directly on the growth and success of the local church, Annual Conference or General Conference and give reports to the pastor, annual bishop or general bishop.

SURVEYS
Will gather district information requested by the Annual or General Conference. Considering these requests as priorities, will strive to follow directions and to meet

deadlines.

INFORMATION DISSEMINATION
Will be official spokesperson for defining the purpose of all programs and services handed down by the Annual or General Conference on the district level. He will direct the distribution of printed materials intended for ministers or local churches.

ACCOUNTING
The District Elder shall give an annual oral report at the Annual Conference, as well as submit in writing, an accounting of the stewardship and financial management of his district. A form for this report will be issued by the Annual Conference from the General Church.

Annual Bishop's Assistance

The Annual Bishop shall schedule a District Elders meeting at least twice a year. However, priority is given to the Annual Bishop to call meetings as often as they deem necessary. These meetings shall focus on a systematic approach to achieving the goals of the Annual and General Conferences. General Conference and General Department Leaders as well as Convention presidents should be invited to attend at least one meeting annually in order to modify approaches to goals, procedures and services.

By-laws of the Union Meeting

1. Every Church shall report to each session of the District Union by letter and delegate.

2. All members of the local church are members of and shall pay dues to the District Union.
3. Every minister, by virtue of their of fine, is a member of and shall pay dues to the District Union.
4. There shall be a District Union Board, consisting of the District Elder, Assistant District Elder, Secretary, Treasurer, and two members at large.
5. The Union Board shall assist the District Elder in all administrative matters of the District Union, when requested to do so.
6. All reports shall be submitted in writing.
7. The Annual Bishop shall have executive power over the District Elder, and shall be responsible to the General Conference for the Union report.
8. Any officer of the District Union, who fails to discharge their duty, shall be removed from office by the District Elder.
9. The Church shall recommend all applicants for Ministerial Certificates and Preacher's Licenses to the District Union. The District Union shall recommend, to the Annual Bishop, all applicants for Preacher's Licenses, Ordination Certificates, and Investigation. These requests must be in writing, and signed by the applicant and authorizing authority. No application will be received by the Conference Board of Examiners or Investigation, without the signature of the Annual Bishop.
10. The District Union shall pay 1/4 of its receipts, raised in each session, for General Funds to the Annual Bishop. Report blanks shall be sent to   all District Elders by the Annual Bishop.
11. The District Union General Funds shall be sent to the Annual Bishop by the District Elder, within five (5) days after the close of the session. The bishop shall

issue an official receipt to the Union and forward a report, within five (5) days, to the General Financial Secretary.

12. Any District Elder, who fails to make their report according to church law, shall be removed from of five by the Annual Bishop.

13. Stationed, full-time churches are granted the option to open their doors on fifth Sundays for public worship. This shall be done according to the wishes of the local church, and not as a mandate from the denomination. Said churches are required to comply with the By-laws of the District Union Meeting.

The Conferences and General Departments

The Annual Conference

The Design of Annual Conference

The Annual Conference is designed to comprise all the churches within the bounds of its district, keeping a common interest and producing unity of sentiment and discipline, to concentrate its strength in the common cause of Christ, our Lord, and by a brotherly interchange of views among its members to promote growth in grace and knowledge of Gospel truth.

All Annual Conferences shall bear the title of the United American Free Will Baptist Denomination, Incorporated and shall be composed of delegates chosen from the churches of the conference district.
Every minister and elected church delegate shall attend the Annual Conference. The privileges, rights and power of lay delegates are most effectively secured by making the laity a party through representation in legislating for better government of the Church; therefore, each church shall have the right to send one elected delegate to the Annual Conference.

Annual Conference Code

1. The officers of an annual conference shall be a bishop, assistant to the bishop, recording secretary,

70

finance secretary, and treasurer. Each officer is to be elected during the session of the conference, to serve for a period of three years, or the interim of the general conference.

2. Every bishop shall use the budget system for the annual conference, and give each pastor, convention, union, and church a budget.

3. The budgets given shall cover the needs prescribed in the general law. Every annual conference that fails to pay its budget without an acceptable excuse, forfeits its right as a member of the U.A.F.W.B. Denomination, and shall be declared out of fellowship. The general conference shall appoint a committee to revoke the license of all the rebellious factions of any annual conference that is out of fellowship.

4. Each annual conference shall have in its record and in its minutes, the names of every church and minister who pays annual assessments.

5. The annual bishop with his annual conference shall be responsible to the general conference for their assigned budget.

6. The bishop of every annual conference shall report his budget to the general financial secretary within ten days after he receives it. Failure to do so shall result in expulsion from office by the general bishop.

7. It shall be the duty of the annual bishop to hold group meetings and inform the pastor, officers, and members of the immediate needs of the connection as they are handed down to him from the general church. These meetings shall be held at such times and places as the annual bishop appoints. The bishop and his cabinet shall give out budgets, suggest programs, and give other information that will encourage and build up the local and general work.

8. The annual conference shall appropriate funds and contribute to its superannuated ministers or the minister's widow, and mission churches, and pay other necessary expense.

9. The annual conference shall have a standing board of council of immediate appeals to try those who appeal a lower ruling. This council's term of office shall extend from one annual conference to another, or until his successor comes into office by the authority of the annual conference.

10. The annual bishop having knowledge of any case of violation by any church or minister in his conference that fails to be dealt with properly according to the rules of the discipline, on the account of negligence or other causes, shall appoint a council of investigators to try the accused within 30 days after he has been informed of the fact.

11. Every annual conference shall have a standing board of examiners to serve from one annual conference to another, who shall examine all applicants for either local license or Elder Credentials.

12. A certificate of approval shall be given each entitled pastor or ordained minister at the close of the annual conference. This certificate is to be furnished by the general bishop from the general conference.

13. The pastor and the church shall be responsible to the annual conference for the budgets assigned, and for failure or violation, they shall be dealt with according to the general law.

14. Any pastor who fails to conform to the orders of the annual conference in regards to his lawful duties as a pastor to pay his budgets, or to keep the faith and practice the Code of Ethics of the U.A.F.W.B. Denomination, shall forfeit his right to pastor.

15. No pastor shall have pastoral charge over more than two churches at the same time.
16. When a minister is charged and is not prosecuted by his membership church or any church which he serves as pastor, the annual bishop of the annual conference of which the offender is a member, on being apprised of the fact, shall file charge immediately and cite the offender to trial at once before the council of intermediate appeals, and the council of appeals shall proceed to prosecute the matter as in other similar cases.
17. It shall be the duty of all annual bishops and presidents of the various conventions to publish an itemized report annually.
18. It shall be the duty of the annual bishop to stay informed of the goals and directions of the general church and to inform all ministers in his charge. To encourage his ministers to support and promote work of the general denomination.
19. Every annual conference shall have an annual minister's conference called by the annual bishop for the purpose of giving information, interpretations, and strengthening the bonds of brotherhood.
20. Every annual conference shall have workshops and institutes annually for its membership and clergy. These sessions should focus on doctrinal unity and practices of the U.A.F.W.B. Church faith.
21. The General Bishop and Annual Bishop are empowered to intervene in a church dispute or conflict on the Annual level by the written request of either side of the conflict.

Order of Business

- Devotionals
- Introductory Sermon
- Introductory Offering
- Holy Communion
- Official Greetings
- Roll Call
- Appointing of Various Committees
- Reports of Committees
- Unfinished Business
- New Business
- Announcements
- Closing

Annual Sunday School Convention

ARTICLE I—NAME
This convention shall be known as the Annual Sunday School Convention.

ARTICLE II—OBJECTIVES
A) To organize a model Sunday school in every church.
B) To aid Christian Education in promoting "Unity Through Spiritual Excellence."
C) To keep our Superintendents up-to-date on new programs and materials that will improve the quality of the lessons and improve the Sunday school.
D) To help the student become more knowledgeable of the Word in order to gain more from the Public

Worship Service, especially the sermon.

E) To support and be responsive to our Annual Conference and Bishop.

ARTICLE III—MEMBERSHIP

1. Membership in this convention shall consist of those who are members of the local auxiliary.
2. All membership dues shall be determined by the convention.
3. No person shall hold an office in the convention who is not a member in good standing in their local auxiliary.
4. Any member who fails to observe or be governed by the rules of the convention shall be dealt with as the convention or annual conference may deem appropriate.
5. All pastors and ministers shall be members of the convention by virtue of their of five, and the Bishop should see that this rule is enforced.

ARTICLE IV—OFFICERS AND TERMS OF OFFICE

1. Elected officers of this convention shall be president, vice president, recording secretary, financial secretary and treasurer.
2. There shall be a trustee board and a program committee appointed by the president subject to the approval of the elected of fixers of the Convention.
3. The Convention shall meet annually. Special meetings may be called by the president as deemed necessary.
4. The president and all secretaries shall be elected for three years. All other officers shall be elected annually.
5. The president is a member of the General

Department by virtue of their office.

6. The president may appoint annual missionaries whom shall serve annually subject to reappointment. The annual missionaries shall be under the supervision of the annual convention.

BY-LAWS

ARTICLE I—DUTIES OF OFFICERS
PRESIDENT
The president shall preside over the convention, will sign orders on the treasurer for money, cast the deciding vote in case of a tie, make appointments and call official meetings when necessary. In case of a vacancy, the president of the department shall have the power to fill the unexpired term.

VICE PRESIDENT
The vice president shall assist the president and shall preside in the absence of or at the request of the president.

RECORDING SECRETARY
The recording secretary shall keep a true and accurate record of the proceedings of the convention, shall assist the president with secretarial assignments for programs and correspondence of the convention and shall assist the financial secretary as necessary and upon request for efficient convention operations.

FINANCIAL SECRETARY
The financial secretary shall keep an accurate record of all finances of the convention both collections and expenditures; and shall write all orders on the treasurer.

TREASURER
The treasurer shall deposit all monies of the convention giving receipts for the same. They shall pay out money only by written order bearing the signatures of both the financial secretary and president.

TRUSTEE BOARD
The trustee board shall manage all the temporal concerns of the convention. They shall guard all property owned by the convention.

PROGRAM COMMITTEE
The Program Committee shall plan programs that will be uplifting and beneficial to the organization. No planned program will be finalized until it has been approved by the president.

ANNUAL MISSIONARY
The Annual Missionary shall visit each church in their district annually, give lectures and advice to help strengthen the work of the convention. The Annual Missionary shall keep a true and accurate record of places visited,
number of miles traveled, lectures given and the amount of funds collected, if applicable. This information shall be submitted to the convention.

ARTICLE II—ORDER OF BUSINESS FOR THE ANNUAL CONVENTION
- Devotion
- Introductory
- Sermon
- Offering
- Official Greetings
- Roll Call and Qualifying of Officers

- Appointing of Various Committees
- Report of Committees
- Report of Annual Missionaries
- Unfinished Business
- New Business
- Announcements
- Closing

ARTICLE III—LAWS FOR THE LOCAL CHURCH AUXILIARY

1. These shall be the following offices in the local auxiliary, superintendent, assistant superintendent, financial secretary, recording secretary and treasurer.
2. Each auxiliary shall bear the name of its church.
3. Elections shall be held annually for all of fixers.
4. Meetings shall be held as often as deemed necessary by the president.
5. Literature for study and discussion shall be obtained through the convention president.
6. Each auxiliary shall report to the annual convention. The budget will be determined by the annual conference.
7. Each pastor shall be responsible to the convention for the budget of their church.
8. The delegate fees shall be set by the convention.
9. Membership dues shall be determined by the auxiliary.
10. Each auxiliary shall report to the convention by letter and delegate.
11. Persons elected as delegates to the convention shall be competent.
12. The Annual Convention has the general oversight over local auxiliaries.

ARTICLE IV—THE DUTIES OF OFFICERS IN THE LOCAL AUXILIARY

PRESIDENT

The President shall preside over the meeting, sign all orders on the treasurer for money, shall cast the deciding vote in case of a tie, make appointments and call official meetings when necessary. In case of a vacancy, the president of the auxiliary shall have the power to fill the unexpired term with the approval of the pastor.

VICE PRESIDENT

The Vice President shall assist the president in a general way. They shall act in the absence of or by the request of the president.

RECORDING SECRETARY

The Recording Secretary shall record the proceedings of the meetings and keep accurate minutes, do all correspondence, and shall assist in a general way as requested by the president.

FINANCIAL SECRETARY

The Financial Secretary shall keep a true and accurate record of all finances of the auxiliary, both collections and expenditures, and shall write all orders on the treasurer.

TREASURER

The Treasurer shall deposit all monies of the auxiliary giving receipt for the same. They shall disburse money only by written orders of the financial secretary, bearing signatures of both the financial secretary and president.

SICK COMMITTEE

The Sick Committee shall bring a written report of all

reported and known sick members.

PROGRAM COMMITTEE
The Program Committee shall plan programs that will be uplifting and beneficial to the organization. No program will be finalized without the approval of the president.

ARTICLE V—LOCAL AUXILIARY ORDER OF BUSINESS
- Devotion
- Scripture Reading
- Prayer
- Hymn
- Minutes of Previous Meeting
- Roll Call
- Unfinished Business
- New Business
- Report of Program Committee
- Report of Sick Committee
- Report of Monies Received and Disbursed
- Benediction

Annual Young People's Christian League Convention

ARTICLE I—NAME
This convention shall be known as the Annual Young People's Christian League Convention—Y.P.C.L.

ARTICLE II—OBJECTIVES
A) To organize a model Young People's Christian League in every church.
B) To teach young people the rules and doctrines of the United American Free Will Baptist Denomination.

C) To give young people an active part in the annual conference.

D) To support the efforts of Christian Education on the annual and general levels.

ARTICLE III—MEMBERSHIP

1. Membership in this convention shall consist of those who are members of the local auxiliary.
2. All membership dues shall be determined by the convention.
3. No person shall hold an office in the convention who is not in good standing in their local auxiliary.
4. Any member who fails to observe or be governed by the rules of the convention shall be dealt with as the convention or annual conference may deem appropriate.
5. All pastors and ministers shall be members of the convention by virtue of their of five, and the Bishop should see that this rule is enforced.

ARTICLE IV—OFFICERS AND TERMS OF OFFICE

1. Elected officers of this convention shall be president, vice president, recording secretary, financial secretary and treasurer.
2. There shall be a trustee board and a program committee appointed by the president subject to the approval of the elected officers of the convention.
3. The Convention shall meet annually. Special meetings may be called by the president as deemed necessary.
4. The president and all secretaries shall be elected for three years. All other of fixers shall be elected annually.
5. The president is a member of the General

Department by virtue of their office.

6. The president may appoint annual missionaries whom shall serve annually subject to reappointment. The annual missionaries shall be under the supervision of the annual convention.

ARTICLE I—DUTIES OF OFFICERS

PRESIDENT
The president shall preside over the convention, will sign orders on the treasurer for money, cast the deciding vote in case of a tie, make appointments and call official meetings when necessary. In case of a vacancy, the president of the department shall have the power to fill the unexpired term.

VICE PRESIDENT
The vice president shall assist the president and shall preside in the absence of or at the request of the president.

RECORDING SECRETARY
The recording secretary shall keep a true and accurate record of the proceedings of the convention; shall assist the president with secretarial assignments for programs and correspondence of the convention and shall assist the financial secretary as necessary and upon request for efficient convention operations.

FINANCIAL SECRETARY
The financial secretary shall keep an accurate record of all finances of the convention both collections and expenditures; and shall write down all orders on the treasurer.

TREASURER
The treasurer shall deposit all monies of the convention giving receipts for the same. They shall pay out money only by written order bearing the signatures of both the financial secretary and president.

TRUSTEE BOARD
The trustee board shall manage all the temporal concerns of the convention. They shall guard all property owned by the convention.

PROGRAM COMMITTEE
The Program Committee shall plan programs that will be uplifting and beneficial to the organization. No planned program will be finalized until it has been approved by the president.

ANNUAL MISSIONARY
The Annual Missionary shall visit each church in their district annually, give lectures and advice to help strengthen the work of the convention. The Annual Missionary shall keep a true and accurate record of places visited, number of miles traveled, lectures given and the amount of funds collected, if applicable. This information shall be submitted to the convention.

ARTICLE II—ORDER OF BUSINESS FOR THE ANNUAL CONVENTION
- Devotion
- Introductory
- Sermon
- Offering
- Official Greetings
- Roll Call and Qualifying of Officers

- Appointing of Various Committees
- Report of Committees
- Report of Annual Missionaries
- Unfinished Business
- New Business
- Announcements
- Closing

ARTICLE III—LAWS FOR THE LOCAL CHURCH AUXILIARY

1. These shall be the following offices in the local auxiliary, president, vice president, financial secretary, recording secretary and treasurer.
2. Each auxiliary shall bear the name of its church.
3. Elections shall be held annually for all of fixers.
4. Meetings shall be held as often as deemed necessary by the president.
5. Literature for study and discussion shall be obtained through the convention president.
6. Each auxiliary shall report to the annual convention. The budget will be determined by the annual conference.
7. Each pastor shall be responsible to the convention for the budget of their church.
8. The delegate fees shall be set by the convention.
9. Membership dues shall be determined by the auxiliary.
10. Each auxiliary shall report to the convention by letter and delegate.
11. Persons elected as delegates to the convention shall be competent.
12. The Annual Convention has the general oversight over local auxiliaries.

ARTICLE IV—THE DUTIES OF OFFICERS IN THE LOCAL AUXILIARY
PRESIDENT

The President shall preside over the meeting, sign all orders on the treasurer for money, shall cast the deciding vote in case of a tie, make appointments and call official meetings when necessary. In case of a vacancy, the president of the auxiliary shall have the power to fill the unexpired term with the approval of the pastor.

VICE PRESIDENT

The Vice President shall assist the president in a general way. They shall act in the absence of or by the request of the president.

RECORDING SECRETARY

The recording secretary shall record the proceedings of the meetings and keep accurate minutes, do all correspondence, and shall assist in a general way as requested by the president.

FINANCIAL SECRETARY

The Financial Secretary shall keep a true and accurate record of all finances of the auxiliary, both collections and expenditures, and shall write all orders on the treasurer.

TREASURER

The treasurer shall deposit all monies of the auxiliary giving receipt for the same. They shall disburse money only by written orders of the financial secretary, bearing signatures of both the financial secretary and president.

SICK COMMITTEE

The Sick Committee shall bring a written report of all

reported and known sick members.

PROGRAM COMMITTEE
The Program Committee shall plan programs that will be uplifting and beneficial to the organization. No program will be finalized without the approval of the president.

ARTICLE V—LOCAL AUXILIARY ORDER OF BUSINESS
- Devotion
- Scripture Reading
- Prayer
- Hymn
- Minutes of Previous Meeting
- Roll Call
- Unfinished Business
- New Business
- Report of Program Committee
- Report of Sick Committee
- Report of Monies Received and Disbursed
  Benediction

Annual Usher's Convention

ARTICLE I—NAME
This convention shall be known as the Annual Usher's Convention

ARTICLE II—OBJECTIVES
A) To give ushers an active part in the Annual Conference.
B) To provide leadership and supervision for local church Usher Boards.
C) To work toward unifying procedures for ushering.
D) To be ready to serve at the request of the annual

bishop or general president.

ARTICLE III—MEMBERSHIP
1. Membership in this convention shall consist of those who are members of the local church Usher Board.
2. All membership dues shall be determined by the convention.
3. No person shall hold an office in the convention who is not in good standing with their local church Usher Board.
4. Any member who fails to be governed by the rules of the convention shall be dealt with as the convention or annual conference may deem appropriate.
5. All pastors and ministers shall be members of the convention by virtue of their of fine, and the Bishop should see that this rule is enforced.

ARTICLE IV—OFFICERS AND TERMS OF OFFICE
1. Elected officers of this convention shall be president, vice president, recording secretary, financial secretary and treasurer.
2. There shall be a trustee board and a program committee appointed by the president subject to the approval of the elected of fixers of the convention.
3. The convention shall meet annually. Special meetings may be called by the president as deemed necessary.
4. The president and all secretaries shall be elected for three years. All other officers shall be elected annually.
5. The president is a member of the General Department by virtue of their office.
6. The president may appoint annual field workers whom shall serve annually subject to reappointment. The annual workers shall be under the supervision of the

annual convention.

ARTICLE I—DUTIES OF OFFICERS
PRESIDENT
The president shall preside over the convention, will sign orders on the treasurer for money, cast the deciding vote in case of a tie, make appointments and call official meetings when necessary. In case of a vacancy, the president of the department shall have the power to fill the unexpired term.

VICE PRESIDENT
The Vice President shall assist the president and shall preside in the absence of or at the request of the president.

RECORDING SECRETARY
The recording secretary shall keep a true and accurate record of the proceedings of the convention, shall assist the president with secretarial
assignments for programs and correspondence of the convention and shall assist the financial secretary as necessary and upon request for efficient convention operations.

FINANCIAL SECRETARY
The financial secretary shall keep an accurate record of all finances of the convention both collections and expenditures, and shall write all orders on the treasurer.

TREASURER
The treasurer shall deposit all monies of the convention giving receipts for the same. They shall pay out money only

by written order bearing the signatures of both the financial secretary and president.

TRUSTEE BOARD
The trustee board shall manage all the temporal concerns of the convention. They shall guard all property owned by the convention.

PROGRAM COMMITTEE
The program committee shall plan programs that will be uplifting and beneficial to the organization. No planned program will be finalized until it has been approved by the president.

ANNUAL FIELD WORKERS
Field workers shall visit churches assigned them by the president, give lectures and advice to help strengthen the work of the conversation. The field worker shall keep a true and accurate record of all places visited, number of miles traveled, lectures given and the amount of any money received. This information shall be submitted to the convention.

ARTICLE IV—THE DUTIES OF OFFICERS IN THE LOCAL AUXILIARY
PRESIDENT
The President shall preside over the meeting, sign all orders on the treasurer for money, shall cast the deciding vote in case of a tie, make appointments and call official meetings when necessary, In case of a vacancy, the president of the auxiliary shall have the power to fill the unexpired term with the approval of the pastor.

VICE PRESIDENT
The Vice President shall assist the president in a general way. They shall act in the absence of or by the request of the president.

RECORDING SECRETARY
The recording secretary shall record the proceedings of the meetings and keep accurate minutes, do all correspondence, and shall assist in a general way as requested by the president.

FINANCIAL SECRETARY
The Financial Secretary shall keep a true and accurate record of all finances of the auxiliary, both collections and expenditures, and shall write all orders on the treasurer.

TREASURER
The treasurer shall deposit all monies of the auxiliary giving receipt for the same. They shall disburse money only by written orders of the financial secretary, bearing signatures of both the financial secretary and president.

SICK COMMITTEE
The Sick Committee shall bring a written report of all reported and known sick members.

PROGRAM COMMITTEE
The Program Committee shall plan programs that will be uplifting and beneficial to the organization. No program will be finalized without the
approval of the president.

ARTICLE V—LOCAL AUXILIARY ORDER OF BUSINESS
- Devotion

- Scripture Reading
- Prayer
- Hymn
- Minutes of Previous Meeting
- Roll Call
- Unfinished Business
- New Business
- Report of Program Committee
- Report of Sick Committee
- Report of Monies Received and Disbursed
- Benediction

Annual Home Mission Convention

ARTICLE I—NAME

This convention shall be known as the Annual Home Mission Convention.

ARTICLE II—OBJECTIVES

A) To organize a Home Mission Department in every church in the conference.

B) To provide supervision of the mission work throughout the annual conference.

C) To strengthen the annual conference financially and spiritually.

D) To assist the annual bishop in meeting the goals of the General Church.

E) To share our love with others by fulfilling the cause of mission which includes teaching and services.

ARTICLE III—MEMBERSHIP

1. Membership in this convention shall consist of those who are members of the local auxiliary.

2. All membership dues shall be determined by the

convention.

3. No person shall hold an office in the convention who is not a member in good standing in their local auxiliary.
4. Any member who fails to observe or be governed by the rules of the convention shall be dealt with as the convention or annual conference may deem appropriate.
5. All pastors and ministers shall be members of the convention by virtue of their of fine, and the Bishop should see that this rule is enforced.

ARTICLE IV—OFFICERS AND TERMS OF OFFICE

1. Elected officers of this convention shall be president, vice president, recording secretary, financial secretary and treasurer.
2. There shall be a trustee board and a program committee appointed by the president subject to the approval of the elected officers of the convention.
3. The convention shall meet annually. Special meetings may be called by the president as deemed necessary.
4. The president and all secretaries shall be elected for three years. All other officers shall be elected annually.
5. The president is a member of the General Department by virtue of their office.
6. The president may appoint annual missionaries whom shall serve annually subject to reappointment. The annual missionaries shall be under the supervision of the annual convention.

BY-LAWS

ARTICLE I—DUTIES OF OFFICERS

PRESIDENT

The president shall preside over the convention, will sign orders on the treasurer for money, cast the deciding vote in case of a tie, make appointments and call official meetings when necessary. In case of a vacancy, the president of the department shall have the power to fill the unexpired term.

VICE PRESIDENT

The vice president shall assist the president and shall preside in the absence of or at the request of the president.

RECORDING SECRETARY

The recording secretary shall keep a true and accurate record of the proceedings of the convention; shall assist the president with secretarial assignments for programs and correspondence of the convention and shall assist the financial secretary as necessary and upon request for efficient convention operations.

FINANCIAL SECRETARY

The financial secretary shall keep an accurate record of all finances of the convention both collections and expenditures; and shall write all orders on the treasurer.

TREASURER

The treasurer shall deposit all monies of the convention giving receipts for the same. They shall pay out money only by written order bearing the signatures of both the financial secretary and president.

TRUSTEE BOARD

The trustee board shall manage all the temporal concerns of the convention. They shall guard all property owned by the convention.

PROGRAM COMMITTEE
The Program Committee shall plan programs that will be uplifting and beneficial to the organization. No planned program will be finalized until it has been approved by the president.

ANNUAL MISSIONARY
The Annual Missionary shall visit each church in their district annually, give lectures and advice to help strengthen the work of the convention. The Annual Missionary shall keep a true and accurate record of places visited, number of miles traveled, lectures given and the amount of funds collected, if applicable. This information shall be submitted to the convention.

ARTICLE II—ORDER OF BUSINESS FOR THE ANNUAL CONVENTION
- Devotion
- Introductory
- Sermon
- Offering
- Official Greetings
- Roll Call and Qualifying of Officers
- Appointing of Various Committees
- Report of Committees
- Report of Annual Missionaries
- Unfinished Business
- New Business
- Announcements
- Closing

ARTICLE III—LAWS FOR THE LOCAL CHURCH AUXILIARY
1. These shall be the following offices in the local

auxiliary, president, vice president, financial secretary, recording secretary and treasurer.

2. Each auxiliary shall bear the name of its church.
3. Elections shall be held annually for all officers.
4. Meetings shall be held as often as deemed necessary by the president.
5. Literature for study and discussion shall be obtained through the convention president.
6. Each auxiliary shall report to the annual convention. The budget will be determined by the annual conference.
7. Each pastor shall be responsible to the convention for the budget of their church.
8. The delegate fees shall be set by the convention.
9. Membership dues shall be determined by the auxiliary.
10. Each auxiliary shall report to the convention by letter and delegate.
11. Persons elected as delegates to the convention shall be competent.
12. The Annual Convention has the general oversight over local auxiliaries.

ARTICLE IV—THE DUTIES OF OFFICERS IN THE LOCAL AUXILIARY
PRESIDENT

The President shall preside over the meeting, sign all orders on the treasurer for money, shall cast the deciding vote in case of a tie, make appointments and call official meetings when necessary. In case of a vacancy, the president of the auxiliary shall have the power to fill the unexpired term with the approval of the pastor.

VICE PRESIDENT
The Vice President shall assist the president in a general way. They shall act in the absence of or by the request of the president.

RECORDING SECRETARY
The recording secretary shall record the proceedings of the meetings and keep accurate minutes, do all correspondence, and shall assist in a general way as requested by the president.

FINANCIAL SECRETARY
The Financial Secretary shall keep a true and accurate record of all finances of the auxiliary, both collections and expenditures, and shall write all orders on the treasurer.

TREASURER
The treasurer shall deposit all monies of the auxiliary giving receipt for the same. They shall disburse money only by written orders of the financial secretary, bearing signatures of both the financial secretary and president.

SICK COMMITTEE
The Sick Committee shall bring a written report of all reported and known sick members.

PROGRAM COMMITTEE
The Program Committee shall plan programs that will be uplifting and beneficial to the organization. No program will be finalized without the approval of the president.

ARTICLE V—LOCAL AUXILIARY ORDER OF BUSINESS
- Devotion Scripture
- Reading Prayer

- Hymn
- Minutes of Previous Meeting
- Roll Call
- Unfinished Business
- New Business
- Report of Program Committee
- Report of Sick Committee
- Report of Monies Received and Disbursed
- Benediction

The Annual Department of Christian Education

ARTICLE I—NAME
This department shall be known as the Annual Department of Christian Education.

ARTICLE II—OBJECTIVES
A) To teach that men may be brought into fellowship with God.
B) To teach that those, thus brought into fellowship can be built up.
C) To teach that after you are brought into fellowship and built up, you can become teachers.

ARTICLE III—MEMBERSHIP
1. Membership in this department shall consist of those who are members of the local department.
2. All membership dues shall be determined by the department.
3. No person shall hold an office in the department who is not a member in good standing in their local department.
4. Any member who fails to observe or be governed by

the rules of the department shall be dealt with as the department or annual conference may deem appropriate.

5. All pastors and ministers shall be members of the department by virtue of their of five, and the Bishop should see that this rule is enforced.

ARTICLE IV OFFICERS AND TERMS OF OFFICE

1. Elected officers of this department shall be director, assistant director, recording secretary, financial secretary and treasurer.
2. There shall be a trustee board and a program committee appointed by the director, subject to the approval of the elected officers of the department.
3. The department shall meet annually. Special meetings may be called by the director as deemed necessary.
4. The director and all secretaries shall be elected for three years. All other officers shall be elected annually.
5. The director is a member of the General Department of Christian Education by virtue of their office.
6. The director may appoint annual missionaries whom shall serve annually subject to reappointment. The annual missionaries shall be under the supervision of the annual department.

BY-LAWS

ARTICLE I—DUTIES OF OFFICERS
DIRECTOR

The director shall preside over the department, will sign orders on the treasurer for money, cast the deciding vote in case of a tie, make appointments and call official meetings when necessary. In case of a vacancy, the director of the department shall have power to fill the unexpired term.

ASSISTANT DIRECTOR
The assistant director shall assist the director and shall preside in the absence of or at the request of the director.

RECORDING SECRETARY
The recording secretary shall keep a true and accurate record of the proceedings of the department; shall assist the director with secretarial assignments for programs and correspondence of the department and shall assist the financial secretary as necessary and upon request for efficient department operations.

FINANCIAL SECRETARY
The financial secretary shall keep an accurate record of all finances of the department both collections and expenditures; and shall write all orders on the treasurer.

TREASURER
The treasurer shall deposit all monies of the department, giving receipts for the same. They shall pay out money only by written order bearing the signatures of both the financial secretary and director.

TRUSTEE BOARD
The trustee board shall manage all the temporal concerns of the department. They shall guard all property owned by the department.

PROGRAM COMMITTEE
The program committee shall plan programs that will be uplifting and beneficial to the department. No planned

program will be finalized until it has been approved by the director.

ANNUAL MISSIONARY

The annual missionary shall visit each church in their district annually, give lectures and advice to help strengthen the work of the department. The annual missionary shall keep a true and accurate record of places visited, number of miles traveled, lectures given and the amount of funds collected, if applicable. This information shall be submitted to the department.

ARTICLE II—ORDER OF BUSINESS FOR THE ANNUAL DEPARTMENT

- Devotion
- Introductory
- Sermon
- Offering
- Official Greetings
- Roll Call and Qualifying of Officers
- Appointing of Various Committees
- Report of Committees
- Report of Annual Missionaries
- Unfinished Business
- New Business
- Announcements
- Closing

ARTICLE III—LAWS FOR THE LOCAL CHURCH DEPARTMENT

1. The following shall be the offices in the local department: director, assistant director, recording secretary, financial secretary, and treasurer.
2. Each department shall bear the name of its church.

3. Elections shall be held annually for all of fixers.
4. Meetings shall be held as often as deemed necessary by the director.
5. Literature for study and discussion shall be obtained through the annual director.
6. Each local department shall report to the annual department. The budget will be determined by the annual department.
7. Each pastor shall be responsible to the annual department for the budget of their church.
8. The delegate fees shall be set by the annual department.
9. Membership dues shall be determined by the local department.
10. Each local department shall report to the annual department by letter and delegate.
11. Persons elected as delegates to the annual department shall be   competent.
12. The annual department has the general oversight over the local departments.

ARTICLE IV—DUTIES OF OFFICERS IN THE LOCAL DEPARTMENT
DIRECTOR

The director shall preside over the department, will sign orders on the treasurer for money, cast the deciding vote in case of a tie, make appointments and call official meetings when necessary. In case of a vacancy, the director of the department shall have power to fill the unexpired term.

ASSISTANT DIRECTOR

The assistant director shall assist the director and shall preside in the absence of or at the request of the director.

RECORDING SECRETARY

The recording secretary shall keep a true and accurate record of the proceedings of the department; shall assist the director with secretarial assignments for programs and correspondence of the department and shall assist the financial secretary as necessary and upon request for efficient department operations.

FINANCIAL SECRETARY

The financial secretary shall keep an accurate record of all finances of the department both collections and expenditures; and shall write all orders on the treasurer.

TREASURER

The treasurer shall deposit all monies of the department, giving receipts for the same. They shall pay out money only by written order bearing the signatures of both the financial secretary and director.

TRUSTEE BOARD

The trustee board shall manage all the temporal concerns of the department. They shall guard all property owned by the department.

PROGRAM COMMITTEE

The program committee shall plan programs that will be uplifting and beneficial to the department. No planned program will be finalized until it has been approved by the director.

ANNUAL MISSIONARY

The annual missionary shall visit each church in their district annually, give lectures and advice to help strengthen the work of the department. The annual missionary shall keep a true and accurate record of places visited, number of miles traveled, lectures given and the amount of funds collected, if applicable. This information shall be submitted to the department.

ARTICLE V—LOCAL DEPARTMENT ORDER OF BUSINESS

- Devotion
- Scripture
- Reading
- Prayer
- Hymn
- Minutes of Previous Meeting
- Roll Call
- Unfinished Business
- New Business
- Report of Program Committee
- Financial Report
- Benediction

The General Organization Chart

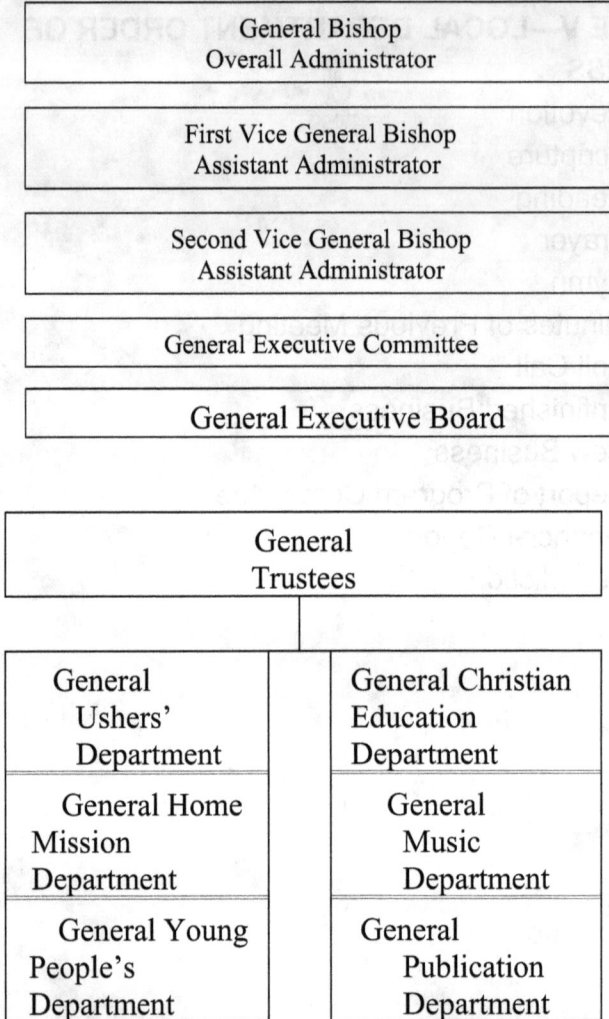

General Bishop
Overall Administrator

First Vice General Bishop
Assistant Administrator

Second Vice General Bishop
Assistant Administrator

General Executive Committee

General Executive Board

General
Trustees

General Ushers' Department	General Christian Education Department
General Home Mission Department	General Music Department
General Young People's Department	General Publication Department

The General Conference

Design of the General Conference

The General Conference is designed to comprise all the annual conferences in the U.A.F.W.B. Denomination, and to complete the organization of the connection—to consolidate the body by harmonizing its different parts, keeping a common interest and producing unity of sentiment and discipline—to concentrate its strength in the common cause of the Redeemer, and, by a fraternal interchange of views among its members to promote growth in grace and knowledge of gospel truth.

The general conference sustains the same relationship to the annual conference as the annual conferences do to the churches of which they are composed.

The annual bishops of the different annual conferences together with their annual conferences are responsible to the general conference for all the general funds levied and raised in the bounds of their conferences; and shall obtain the general bishop's certificate of approval before serving in the annual bishop's office.

Section II

Constitution and By-laws of the General Conference

- **Article 1.** This conference shall be called the general conference of the United American Free Will Baptist Denomination, Incorporated and shall be composed of the general officers, general boards, the various bishops, and presidents of annual conventions, the legal delegates from the annual conferences and conventions, churches, and ordained ministers.

- **Article 2.** Any annual conference may be received as a body into this conference by a two-thirds vote of the members present at any regular session. It shall be the duty of the annual conference to report themselves by delegation and letter to each session of the general conference giving in their letters and statistics. Any annual conference may be received in the general conference by a majority vote of the general conference.
- **Article 3.** Each annual conference belonging to this general conference shall be entitled to representation by one delegate to every five hundred members or however shall be decided by the general conference.
- **Article 4.** The stated sessions of this conference shall be held once in three years, to commence on the third Wednesday in June, at eleven o'clock AM at the General Church Tabernacle.
- **Article 5.** Extra sessions may be called or the time between sessions lengthened, by the general bishop or two-thirds of the elective of firers.
- **Article 6.** The of fixers of this conference shall be a general bishop, first vice general bishop, second vice general bishop, recording secretary, financial secretary, treasurer, executive board chairman, trustee board chairman, auditor, editor, and parliamentarian. Said of fixers to be elected by a majority vote during each session of this conference and shall hold their office for three years.

- **Article 7.** It shall be the duty of the general bishop to preside during his term of office with prudence and piety, laboring all the while to further the gospel, and to the building up of the denomination in general. He shall have frequent interviews with the annual bishops and shall see that all things work together for good. He shall be responsible for the execution and promotion of the doctrine, rules, and regulations of the general church. He is an ex of ficio member of all annual conferences, conventions, boards, and committees of the U.A.F.W.B. Denomination.
- **Article 8.** It shall be the duty of the recording secretary to (1) record the names of all the delegates elect to the ensuing general conference which names shall be sent immediately after their election by the clerk of the annual conference. (2) To record the proceedings of the ensuing general conference. (3) To take charge of the books, papers, deeds, bonds, and other property belonging to the general conference not otherwise provided for.
- **Article 9.** It shall be the duty of the general financial secretary to receive and make record of all monies coming into the general church. Said funds are then to be deposited with the general treasurer who shall furnish a receipt therefore. The general financial secretary shall keep an account of all disbursements and know the financial status of the general church at all times. The general financial secretary shall be bonded.
- **Article 10.** The treasurer shall keep a true account of all monies or other valuables that may come into his possession. He shall keep a clear account of all money received and give an account of all monies disbursed. He shall keep the money in a bank in

Kinston, North Carolina (to be decided by the executive committee) in the name of the UNITED AMERICAN FREE WILL BAPTIST CHURCH, INC. He shall be properly bonded and his records shall be subject to inspection at all times. He shall issue checks upon authorization by requisition from the general bishop who shall have received orders from the trustee board.

- **Article 11.** The assistant officers shall perform the duties usually devolving upon such officers.
- **Article 12.** The executive board which shall consist of the annual bishops, the elective officers of the conference, members appointed and approved by the annual bishop, shall have the power to adopt rules needful for its own government, and to carry out plans to understandings of the conference, make contracts, employ agents, and exercise all the functions of the general conference not repugnant with its rules, regulations and directions.
- **Article 13.** The executive board shall keep a true and faithful record of all its proceedings, and make a full report at each regular session of the conference, and be subject to and comply with all directions, requests, and regulations of the general conference. The executive board shall be members ex officio of the general conference.
- **Article 14.** The general board of trustees shall consist of not less than seven persons. Each member shall be not less than twenty-one years of age and members in good standing in the United American Free Will Baptist Denomination.
- **Article 15.** The board of trustees shall be responsible to the executive board and shall be required to present a report of its acts annually to the executive

- **Article 16.** No person who is a trustee shall be ejected from office while he is personally responsible for money except where it is deemed advisable by the executive committee.
- **Article 17.** It shall be the duty of the trustee board to take charge and protect the church property, with all its appurtenances, in trust for the membership, and to make such improvements as may be necessary from time to time for the interest of the Society of which they are trustees; and to see that order and decorum are at all times observed in the general conference.
- **Article 18.** The executive committee shall see that the treasurer and financial secretary makes the bond required.
- **Article 19.** There shall be an executive committee composed of all elective officers of the general conference and the president of each general department. This committee shall perform the duties of the executive board except the regular annual board meeting.

  Article 19—A. It shall be the duty of the parliamentarian to rule on parliamentary questions that might arise only during a business session. These rulings must be in accord with Robert's Rules of Order which shall be the authority on all questions of procedure not specifically stated in this constitution and by-laws.
- **Article 20.** Each session of the general conference shall be called to order by the general bishop. The first and second vice general bishop should be permitted to preside over sessions of the general conference, as the general bishop deems proper.

- **Article 21.** Each session and adjournment of the general conference shall be opened and closed by singing and praying.
- **Article 22.** Thirty-five members shall be required to constitute a quorum to transact business of the general conference.
- **Article 23.** After the opening of each session of the general conference, the general bishop shall appoint a committee of not less than three persons to examine the credentials for membership in the conference. After the report of this committee and enrollment of members present the conference shall proceed to the transaction of business.
- **Article 24.** At each session of the general conference, standing committees shall be appointed on such subjects as follows: Education, Temperance, Necrology, Ethics, Petition, and Requests. All petitions and requests and documents on particular subjects shall be referred to their appropriate committees. Special committees may be appointed at the pleasure of the conference.
- **Article 25.** This conference shall sit with open doors except when it is necessary to go into executive session. Then only legal representatives may be permitted in the auditorium.
- **Article 26.** Any person not a member of the general conference may be allowed to take part in the discussions by obtaining permission of the general conference except when in executive session.
- **Article 27.** It shall be the duty of the recording secretary to furnish each session of the general conference with minutes of the previous session.
- **Article 28.** The general conference may determine the time when its daily sessions shall open and close.

- **Article 29**. It shall be the duty of all the members of the general conference to be present at the time appointed for each daily session, and any one who wishes to retire shall first obtain permission from the general bishop.
- **Article 30.** No member shall be absent from the conference during its session without first obtaining permission from the conference.
- **Article 31.** Any member who wishes to speak in the conference shall first address the general bishop.
- **Article 32.** No person shall be allowed to speak more than twice on any one subject without permission from the conference.
- **Article 33.** No whispering nor interruptions shall be allowed in conference without permission from the bishop. All members shall pay strict attention to the business of the conference.
- **Article 34.** No person shall be allowed to nominate more than one person on any committee, if the person nominated is elected.
- **Article 35.** The type of voting shall be determined by the desires of the conference.
- **Article 36.** The part of the constitution which relates to the general conference shall be read in each session near its opening.
- **Article 37.** The program and other matters pertaining to the general conference shall be prepared by the Executive Committee and the general bishop. All committee members shall be called in plenty of time to prepare a constructive program.
- **Article 38.** The auditor shall make a careful examination of the treasurer's and secretary's accounts and vouchers annually. He shall submit the same to the executive board, or executive committee

when in session.

- **Article 39.** The books shall be at all times subject to the inspection of the general bishop.

General Conference Laws

1. The general conference shall have supervision of all license, and all license shall bear the seal of the general conference and the seal of the annual conference of which holder is a member.

2. The general claims of each annual conference shall be forwarded to the general financial secretary within ten days after its collection by the annual bishop and each annual secretary, and a general receipt issued for the full amount sent. The financial secretary shall immediately deposit such funds with the general treasurer.

3. Every annual conference that fails to comply with the financial demands of the general law, forfeits its interest in the U.A.F.W.B. Church, and shall be declared out of fellowship; and the general conference shall appoint a committee to revoke the license of all the rebellious faction of any dismembered annual conference.

4. The bishop of each annual conference shall be a member of the general conference by virtue of his office, and shall hold office for a term of three years or until the next general conference.

5. A certificate of approval shall be given the annual bishop at the close of the general conference. The general bishop shall prepare these certificates in accordance with the discipline of the church.

6. The general headquarters of the general conference

shall be at Kinston, North Carolina.

7. All general of fixers salaries shall be fixed by the executive committee.
8. A board of missions shall be established and shall conform to the rules of the general conference. Missionaries shall be paid only from mission and church extension funds.
9. The book of discipline shall prescribe some laws and regulations to govern all annexes of the general church.
10. Any regular ordained minister in good standing in the U.A.F.W.B. Church shall have an absolute right to pastor any church in any conference of the general church when he shall have been elected by a majority vote of that church.
11. All the annual conventions shall be subject to the annual conference within whose bounds they exist, and they shall represent to the general conference through the annual conference such amounts as have been assigned.
12. The fees of an annual conference to the general conference shall be levied in accordance with the membership of said conference by the general bishop.
13. If any annual bishop fails to report the monies of his annual conference, union meetings or other general funds, or, if he fails to give written financial reports to the executive committee, he shall forfeit his right to office, unless he is lawfully excused by the executive committee of the general conference.
14. Each annual conference shall labor to promote the cause of mission and education.
15. The general conference shall make such by-laws and regulations, not repugnant to this constitution, as it

may deem necessary.

16. There shall be elected by the general conference a managing editor of publications. The work of this of fine shall be to carry on the publications of the Advocate and other literature with the revenue provided for it. The officers of the publishing department shall make their report to the executive board in each session, and to the general conference.

17. The managing editor of publications shall be paid a salary and shall be under the direction and supervision of the general bishop and the Executive board.

18. The general conference shall issue a general budget sufficient to take care of the general church. The budget shall be issued annually. This budget shall be distributed to the general churches that are under our jurisdiction by the executive committee of the general conference through the annual bishops, in churches and other auxiliaries.

19. The compiler of general matters shall submit his manuscript or minutes on revision work to the general executive committee and the committee shall look after the printing account and other matters related thereto.

20. The general conference shall have power to purchase lands for church and school sites and other benevolent and charitable purposes, and shall have the right to buy and sell, to receive and convey lands, deeds, bonds, notes, papers, etc., in fee simple; defend and prosecute the same at common law when such proposals have been submitted and approved by the executive board in regular session, or the executive committee.

21. The general conference shall have the right to a

common seal.

22. The general conference shall have power to set off annual conferences, in such places and at such times as it may deem best, and appoint a supervisor or bishop to the district if there be not one already appointed, who shall take charge of the district until a bishop is elected.

23. The general conference shall have the power to make new laws, and to revise those already made whenever it shall find it needful for the general good of the connection, and all such laws shall become valid immediately after their sanction by this body. This power is reserved to the annual conference.

24. The general conference shall have the sole right to ask contributions of annual conferences, churches, and individuals and to appropriate to the annual conferences a due ratio of said amount necessary to prosecute the denominational work. Gifts, bequests to the various denominational societies shall transfer their work to the conference.

25. The general bishop shall have the authority to appoint individuals to work to extend the borders of the denominational bounds, to expand programs and services of the general conference.

26. Each annual conference belonging to the general conference shall be subject to all the rules and directions of the general conference.

27. The general conference approves efforts promoting the cause of education and pledges its undivided support to such as aim for the glory of God, the good of the church, and the welfare of man.

28. It shall be the duty of the general conference to receive and act upon communications from the annual conferences properly belonging to this   body,

to exercise general supervision in all matters for the best interest of the United American Free Will Baptist Denomination.

29. No person in the general conference shall be recognized as an officer or member after he has been silenced or expelled by the executive board. Anyone who does so shall be immediately called and tried by the executive committee. The action of the executive committee will be binding and final.

Eligibility to Hold a General Officer's Position

To be eligible to hold the office of General Bishop or a Vice General Bishop, the person must have been a bonafide, ordained minister in the United American Free Will Baptist Denomination for at least ten consecutive years. Fully believing in and accepting the doctrine, principles and precepts of the denomination. Candidates must have shown interest in all General Departments and programs by attendance and financial support.

To be eligible to hold any of the other General of fines or positions, the candidate must likewise have been a bonafide member of the denomination for at least five consecutive years, fully believing in the doctrine, principles and precepts. Must have also shown interest for the departments and programs by attendance and financial support.

Each candidate for a general office must be in "good standing" in accordance with the adopted rules of the United American Free Will Baptist Denomination.

Election of General Officers

The election for General Officers in the United American Free Will Baptist Denomination takes place every three years during the setting of the General Conference. Officers to be elected are: Bishop, First Vice Bishop, Second Vice Bishop, Recording Secretary, Financial Secretary, Treasurer, Auditor, Executive Board Chairman, Trustee Board Chairman, Editor, Parliamentarian, President of the Home Mission Department, President of the Young People's Department, and President of the Ushers Department. Chairman of the Christian Education, and Music Departments shall be appointed by the Bishop, subject to the approval of the Executive Committee.

When an officer desires to be re-selected or a member to become a candidate for any position in the General Conference, they shall be expected to file a written request with the Executive Board at the Annual Board meeting prior to the General Conference. If a position lacks a written request after the deadline, the Executive Board shall provide a list of recommended nominees from which the qualified delegates would be given the opportunity to vote to fill the position. The majority role will be final.

If, after having been duly elected to an official position in the General Conference, the officer expires or resigns before the term ends, the General Bishop shall be empowered to appoint someone to serve for the remainder of the term. This shall be subject to the approval of the Executive Board.

Guidelines for Holding a General Election

In order to keep suspicions and confusion to a minimum during an election in the General Conference, the following guidelines are the order:

1. In any contested position, each candidate shall have the right to appoint one person to count votes. The Executive Board shall employ three non-Free Will Baptist persons, who have no vested interested in the outcome of the election. These persons shall constitute the Tallying Committee and their report shall be official and final.

2. The tallied results shall be reported by one member of the committee to the secretary in writing on a report form prepared and approved by the Executive Board, bearing the signatures of the members of the Tallying Committee. The secretary shall read orally the results of the committee to the general body.

3. In the case of a non-contested position, after presenting the candidate to the body, the presiding officer shall declare the candidate elected and the office filled. This report shall also be reported to the secretary in writing bearing the signature of the presiding officer.

The General Conference Duties and Status of Officers

The General Bishop

The General Bishop must be a man with all evidence of a Christian. He should be regenerated, sanctified, and filled with the Holy Ghost. He must have been a member of the United American Free Will Baptist Denomination at least ten years prior to election. He must be a man with at least a high school education, demonstrated administrative ability and have desires for continuous educational development. He must be a lover of the church and a lover of people, with the ability to get along well with all people.

A) The General Bishop shall be a consecrated Bishop of the United American Free Will Baptist Denomination; elected by the general conference in session every three years. He shall be the chief Administrative Officer of the General Church. In this capacity, he shall be responsible for the execution and promotion of the doctrine, rules, and regulations of the General Church. He is an ex officio member of all annual conferences, conventions, boards, and committees of the United American Free Will Baptist Denomination. The general bishop should know the doctrine, organization, constitution, and by-laws of the General denomination.

B) The General Bishop should plan at least one visit to each annual conference yearly. He shall obtain and keep records in the General office, all data of annual conferences, conventions, etc. which will include all financial records and other vital statistics. When necessary, the General Bishop may review rulings of presiding officers of annual conferences, conventions, and departments. His ruling in such matters shall be binding until the next general conference. The signature of the general bishop shall appear on each ministerial license and other legal documents of importance of the general church. He shall with the counsel of the Executive Committee and vote of the general church be authorized to organize new conferences when feasible. He shall provide a certificate of transferral of a church from one conference to another providing there is a majority vote of each conference official board and a majority vote of the membership of the church in transfer.

C) The General Bishop in case of a vacancy in the office of annual bishop shall authorize the Assistant to the bishop to assume the duties of the unexpired term. However, an exception to this rule can be made by the discretion of the general bishop.

D) The General Bishop may engage in pastoral work so long as this service does not interfere with the operation of his General Church duties and progress of the local church. As a pastor, he shall be subject to all rules and obligations of a pastor.

E) The General Bishop shall handle no monies except in such cases that may be approved by the Executive Committee.

F) It shall be the general bishop's duty to travel the field, supervise the work in a general way, encourage and inform the people of the church's program, build up the work and promote the educational interests of the general church. He shall keep a complete record of his work and travels, and also report to each session of the Executive Board and the Executive Committee.

G) The General Bishop shall have supervision over all

the annual conferences of the general conference, and the general properties in trust of the U.A.F.W.B. church in accordance with general conference rules.

H) The General Bishop and Annual Bishop are empowered to intervene in a church dispute or conflict on the Annual level by the written request of either side of the conflict.

The First Vice General Bishop

The First Vice General Bishop shall preside in the absence of or at the request of the General Bishop. He shall perform any duties that may be assigned to him by the General Bishop.

The Second Vice General Bishop

The Second Vice General Bishop shall assist the General Bishop as needed. He may perform any duties of the office that may be assigned by the General Bishop.

General Recording Secretary

The general Recording Secretary is the recording of finer of the General Conference and the custodian of its records. His records are to be made available to any superior of finer upon request. His duties are to record the proceedings of the meetings and to keep record of the official activity of the church. He shall preserve all resolutions passed in the general meetings and be able to bring same to the attention of the presiding officer. He shall keep a roll of members of the Executive Board and to call the roll when required; to notify officers, committees, and delegates of their appointment and to furnish committees with all papers referred to them, etc.

General Financial Secretary

The General Financial Secretary shall receive and make record of all monies coming into the general church. Said funds are then to be deposited with the treasurer who shall furnish a receipt
The Financial Secretary shall keep an account of all disbursements and know the financial status of the General Church at all times.

General Treasurer

The General Treasurer shall receive from the Financial Secretary all money belonging to the General church and deposit the same. He shall keep a clear account of all money received, and give an account of all monies disbursed. He shall keep the money in a bank account in the name of the United American Free Will Baptist Church, Inc. (In Kinston, North Carolina) unless otherwise approved by the general conference. He shall be properly bonded and his records shall be subject to inspection at all times. He shall issue checks upon authorization by requisition from the general bishop or Trustee Board.

General Auditor

The auditor shall make a careful examination of the treasurer's and secretary's accounts and vouchers annually. He will submit his findings to the Executive Board, or the Executive Committee when it is in session.

The General Board of Trustees

It is the duty of the Board of Trustees to take charge and protect the general church, and all property with all its appurtenances, in trust for the connection and make such improvements as may be necessary from time to time for the interest of the Society of which they are trustees; and to see that order and decorum are at all times observed in the general conference. They shall be responsible to the executive board and shall be required to present a report of its acts annually when called upon to do so by the Executive Board. The following should be included in the Trustee's Annual Report:

1. Value of General Church Property
2. Amount paid on mortgage
3. Amount paid on floating debts
4. Amount paid on repairs
5. Amount paid on salaries
6. Amount paid on Board Expense
7. Amount paid on all purposes
8. Balance in treasury
9. Present indebtedness
10. Recommendations

The Chairman of the Trustee Board

The Trustee Board Chairman shall preside over the meetings of the Trustee Board and shall have such powers as granted to any other president usually devolving upon such officer.

The Executive Board

The Executive Board will consist of the Annual Bishops,

elective officers, and appointees approved by annual bishops as their official representatives (allotment shall be according to the board's decision). They shall have power to adopt rules needful for its own government, contract, employ agents, authorize the execution of legal papers, collect and appropriate funds, and exercise all the functions of the general conference not repugnant with its rules, regulations, and directions. The Executive Board shall keep a true and faithful record of all its proceedings, and make a full report at each regular session of the conference, and be subject to and comply with all directions, requests, and regulations of the general conference.

The Executive Board Chairman

The Executive Board Chairman shall preside over the meetings of the Executive Board and shall have such powers as granted to any other chairman usually devolving upon such officer.

The Parliamentarian

The Parliamentarian is to be an authority on accepted Parliamentary procedures. His duty is to rule on Parliamentary questions that might arise during a business session as are in accord with Robert's Rules of Order.

Trial Of General Officers

In the Interim of Conference—Appeals

1. Should any of finer of the general conference, other than the executive board and educational board become disqualified during the interim of the general conference, the executive board of being apprised of the fact, shall call the offender to account and after suitable labor if unsuccessful, shall silence the offender for a limited time, or expel from office as the case may be, and appoint another in his stead.

2. Should any member of the executive board become disqualified, the remaining qualified members of said board shall call the offender to account, and after suitable labor, if unsuccessful, shall silence the offender for a limited time or expel from office as the case may be and appoint another in his stead.

3. Should any minister fail to adhere to and defend the discipline, rules, by-laws, resolutions, and directions of the general conference, he shall be brought to trial before the proper authorities and make amends for such offense. Should the offender, after suitable labors fail to concede to the decision of the said authority, his license shall be revoked and he be declared no member of the U.A.F.W.B. Denomination.

4. It is the duty of the general conference on the second day of its session to elect from among its members present five elders, who shall be men of prudence and piety, and possessing a true knowledge of our Book of Discipline, who shall be called Council of Final Appeals. They shall constitute a council of appeal for churches, ministers, officers, and all other

causes that have been found guilty by the decision of the annual conference. A majority shall be competent to decide the case. They shall elect a clerk, and the first named shall preside as chairman. The clerk of the council of appeals shall keep a faithful record of all the proceedings and read the report to the conference. The conference may accept or reject the report.

5. In all cases where an appeal is tried the appellant shall state the grounds of his appeal by council or otherwise. After the case has been truly investigated, the council of final appeals shall examine the case and make such recommendations as it deems just and fair.

6. The general executive committee is hereby constituted a council of final appeals for the annual conference, and the connection in general, in all cases that cannot be decided otherwise. The decision of the executive committee in all matters coming before it properly, shall be binding and final.

General Boards and Departments

1. The general executive board shall publish an itemized report of all their transactions annually for the benefit of the connection in general.
2. The general trustee board shall publish an itemized report of all their transactions annually for the benefit of the connection in general.
3. The general departments shall publish an itemized report of all their transactions annually for the benefit of the connection in general.

General Department of Christian Education

Mission—Purpose

Our Lord's command, "Go...and teach," made Christian Education mandatory. Implicit to His command are three aims:

1. To teach that men may be brought into fellowship with God.
2. To teach that those thus brought into fellowship can be built up.
3. To teach that after you are brought into fellowship and built up, you can become teachers.

True Christian Education is not something of interest to a few people engaged in a particular movement belonging to some organization. No single group of people have a monopoly upon Christian truth. The term "Christian" is rightfully applied to any and every person, church, denomination organization, institution, and movement that is true to the plain, simple teachings of the Bible. The doctrines enunciated originally by the majority of Protestant churches are in accord with such teachings. All who today accept these doctrines probably agree that the aims of Christian Education rest upon meanings and values such as the following: God is the Creator and the Sustainer of the universe which show forth His handiwork; God, a personal and moral Being, created man as a personal and moral being in His own image, responsible for his conduct, so the fear of the Lord is the beginning of wisdom. In Adam man sinned, so all men are sinners by nature and in deed, under the wrath of God and the condemnation of eternal death. God is His infinite love provided in Christ, His own Son, salvation for all who by simple faith accept the righteousness thus made available. The Bible is God's revelation of Himself and His will given men that they may become alive in Him through Christ by the power of the Holy Spirit.

Upon those who have come to know God, rests the responsibility of making known to others the grace of God that they also may, by the Holy Spirit come to experience God through faith in Christ.

Our Concept

"Unity Through Spiritual Excellence"

IN WORSHIP AND PRAISE:
Obedience to God's will and purpose for having made us. Worship and Praise is not something we do because we feel like it. It is an expressed command by God Himself. "Thou shall worship the Lord thy God, and him only shall thou serve" (Matthew 4:10).

IN PURPOSE AND PROCEDURES:

To understand why and to follow through in an orderly manner. "Gather the people together, men and women, and children, and the stranger that is within thy gates, that they may hear, and that they may learn" (Deuteronomy 31: 12).

IN DUTY AND RESPONSIBILITY:
To be depended upon to do that which is expected of us "And he that taketh not his cross and followeth me is not worthy of me" (Matthew 10:38). Whether we want to or not is not the question. "Teaching them to observe all things whatsoever I have commanded you" (Matthew 28:20).

IN LOVE AND UNDERSTANDING:
Exemplifying the Spirit of God. "By this shall all men know that ye are my disciples, if ye have love one to another" (John 13:35), and the wisdom of God (...If ye continue in my Word, then are ye my disciples indeed, and ye shall know the truth, and the truth shall make you FREE" (John 8:31, 32).

ARTICLE I—NAME
The name of this department shall be known as The General Department of Christian Education.

ARTICLE II—OBJECTIVES
1. To establish a Board of Christian Education in the General Church and in each Annual Conference and Church.
2. To assist in defining our educational objectives.
3. To create a comprehensive educational program for our denomination.
4. To promote the importance of Christian Education.

ARTICLE III—DIRECTOR

The General Bishop shall appoint the Director of Christian Education, subject to the approval of the General Executive Committee. The term of office shall be the same as other elected general officials.

The Director of Christian Education shall have direction and supervision over all religious interests of the church, local, annual and general levels subject to the approval of the bishops, pastors, and boards. Must seek to unify and promote Christian Education at each level of the church. The Director shall be a radiant and devout Christian and an active member of the church in which they are a member. Some training in administration would be helpful but not required.

Optimistic, forward looking, courage of spiritual adventure, loves people, loves the job, and has other leadership qualities. Able and willing to experiment and adapt new plans when proven successful by experiments. Must be a conversant, sympathetic with purposes and methods. Humble in spirit of love and with understanding.

ARTICLE IV—STAFF AND EXECUTIVE BOARD POSITIONS

General bishop, general director, associate director, liaison vice president, secretary/treasurer, record keeping committee, chaplain, parliamentarian, public relations/publications, program chairpersons, awards committee, video photography technicians, historians, ministry chairpersons.

The General Home Mission Department

ARTICLE I—NAME

This department shall be known as the General Home Mission Department.

MISSION STATEMENT

It is the mission of the General Home Mission Department of the United American Free Will Baptist Denomination, Inc., to continue to carry out the Great Commission by reaching out to individuals with Special Needs and by doing so spread the Good News to today's youth, to those who are sick at home and in the hospital; to homeless persons, and to those in the nursing home.

ARTICLE II—OBJECTIVES

A) To provide supervision of the mission work throughout the denomination.

B) To strengthen the whole denomination by fulfilling a responsibility that Christ placed upon His Church.

X) To carry the Good News of the Gospel of Jesus Christ to those who cannot come to the Lord's House to receive it.

Δ) To serve those who are in deed.

ARTICLE III—MEMBERSHIP

1. Any person can be a member of this Department upon payment of dues provided they are a bonafide member of a local Free Will Baptist Church in this denomination.

2. All membership dues shall be determined by the department.

3. No person shall hold a position in the department who is not in good standing in their Annual Convention.
4. Any member who fails to observe or be governed by the rules of the department shall not be in good standing with the department.
5. All annual and local of firers are members of the department by virtue of their office. All bishops and executive officers of the denomination are members of the department by virtue of their of fine and shall pay membership dues.

ARTICLE IV—OFFICERS AND TERMS OF OFFICE
1. Elected officers of this department shall Bose president, vice president, recording secretary, financial secretary, treasurer and a trustee board.
2. The department shall meet annually. Special meetings may be called by the president as deemed necessary.
3. All officers shall be elected annually. In case of a death or resignation, the president shall have the power to make an appointment to the office until the next election.
4. The president may appoint missionaries whom shall serve for three years. The missionaries shall be under the supervision of the department.
5. Each annual convention shall report to the general department.
6. One day (Friday) in each session of the general conference shall be set aside for the General Home Mission Department.

BY-LAWS

ARTICLE I—DUTIES OF OFFICERS

PRESIDENT
The president shall preside over the convention, will sign orders on the treasurer for money, cast the deciding vote in case of a tie, make appointments and call official meetings when necessary. In case of a vacancy, the president of the department shall have the power to fill the unexpired term.

VICE PRESIDENT
The vice president shall assist the president and shall preside in the absence of or at the request of the president.

RECORDING SECRETARY
The recording secretary shall keep a true and accurate record of the proceedings of the convention; shall assist the president with secretarial
assignments for programs and correspondence of the convention and shall assist the financial secretary as necessary and upon request for efficient convention operations.

FINANCIAL SECRETARY
The financial secretary shall keep an accurate record of all finances of the convention both collections and expenditures; and shall write all orders on the treasurer.

TREASURER
The treasurer shall deposit all monies of the convention giving receipts for the same. They shall pay out money only by written order bearing the signatures of both the financial

secretary and president.

TRUSTEE BOARD
The trustee board shall manage all the temporal concerns of the convention. They shall guard all property owned by the convention.

General Church Music Department

ARTICLE I—NAME
This organization shall be known as the Music Department of the United American Free Will Baptist Denomination.

ARTICLE II—OBJECTIVES
A) To educate the United American Free Will Baptist Denomination in the different types and the usage of music in the worship service.
B) To educate on the importance of music in the church.
C) To educate the church in the structure and theory of music.
D) To aid in establishing Music Departments within the General Church.
E) To promote unification with equal representation from all Conferences through the General Church Tabernacle Choir.

ARTICLE III—OFFICERS AND TERMS OF OFFICE
A) Officers of this department shall be chairman, vice chairman, secretary, treasurer and chaplain and they shall each serve for a period of three years.
B) There shall be an executive committee composed of all elected officers and an Executive Board which will include all elected officers, appointed of fixers,

134

appointed chairmen and field workers.

ARTICLE IV—MEMBERSHIP AND DUES
1. Any person who is a member of an organized and recognized church upon payment of dues and at least 15 years of age can be a member of the General Tabernacle Choir.
2. Dues shall be affixed by the Executive Committee of the Department and a member must be in good standing financially in order to be a voting member.

ARTICLE V—MEETINGS
1. There shall be at least one scheduled meeting yearly for the General Music Department and the annual conference music departments.
2. Special meetings shall be held at the discretion of the chairman.

BY-LAWS

ARTICLE I—DUTIES OF OFFICERS
CHAIRMAN
The Chairman shall preside over the session, sign all orders on the treasurer for money, and shall cast the deciding vote in case of a tie, make appointments, and call official meetings when necessary.

VICE CHAIRMAN
The vice chairman shall assist the chairman in a general way. The vice chairman shall preside in the absence of or at the request of the chairman. The vice chairman shall assist the chairman in planning and arranging all programs.

SECRETARY

The secretary shall keep accurate minutes of all meetings, and do all correspondence required by the department. The secretary shall keep an accurate record of all finance of the department, both collection and expenditures, and write all orders on the treasurer. The secretary shall assist the chairman in planning and arranging all programs.

TREASURER

The treasurer shall hold all monies of the department. Upon request give official receipt of collection and pay out by written orders signed by the chairman and secretary. The treasurer shall assist the chairman in planning and arranging all programs.

CHAPLAIN

The Chaplain shall be responsible for the devotional activities conducted at each regular meeting. The chaplain shall assist the chairman in a general way. The chaplain shall assist the chairman in planning and arranging all programs.

THE EXECUTIVE COMMITTEE

The Executive Committee shall be composed of all elected officers of the General Music Department. They shall have the authority to conduct all business which shall arise between regular meetings and shall make a report of their actions to the membership. The decision of the Executive Committee in all matters coming before it properly shall be binding and final.

THE EXECUTIVE BOARD

This board shall consist of all elected of fixers, appointed chairmen and field workers. They shall work to enhance the programs of the department and to insure that the general body is informed of the objectives and goals of the department.

THE APPOINTED CHAIRMEN AND FIELD WORKERS
The appointed chairmen and field workers shall attend all meetings when requested and report back to their annual conferences. Each annual conference shall report to the General Music Department.

The General Usher's Department

ARTICLE I—NAME
This organization shall be known as the General Usher's Department of the United American Free Will Baptist Denomination, Inc.

ARTICLE II—OBJECTIVES
A) To provide leadership and general supervision for Annual Usher Conventions.
B) To unify the procedures of ushering in the General Church.
C) To strengthen the bonds of Christian unity and fellowship.
D) To endeavor to cause all people within our influence to be a worshiper while in church.
E) To assist in promoting a spiritual atmosphere that would enable the minister to carry on a type of worship that would divinely inspire the worshipers.

ARTICLE III—MEMBERSHIP
Any person can be a member of this Department upon payment of dues provided they are a bonafide member of a

local Free Will Baptist Church in this denomination.

ARTICLE IV—OFFICERS
The officers of this organization shall be president, vice president, recording secretary, financial secretary, treasurer, and trustee board.

BY-LAWS

ARTICLE I—DUTIES AND TERMS OF OFFICE
- **Section 1.** All officers shall hold office for a period of three years. In case of a vacancy, the president of the department shall have power to fill the unexpired term.
- **Section 2.** The president shall preside at all meetings. He shall appoint all committees and shall be an ex officio member of all committees.
- **Section 3.** The vice president shall assist the president and shall preside in the absence of or at the request of the president.
- **Section 4.** The recording secretary shall keep a true and accurate record of the proceedings of the Department, shall assist the president with secretarial assignments for programs and correspondence of the department and shall assist the financial secretary as necessary and upon request, for efficient department operations.
- **Section 5.** The financial secretary shall keep a true and accurate record of all finances of the department both of collections and expenditures, and shall write all orders on the treasured
- **Section 6.** The treasurer shall deposit all monies of the department giving receipts for the same. They

shall pay out money only by written order bearing the signatures of both the financial secretary and president.

- **Section 7.** The trustee board shall manage all the temporal concerns of the department. They shall guard all property owned by the department.

ARTICLE II—COMMITTEES

1. **Section 1.** Special committees will be appointed by the president as they are needed.
2. **Section 2.** Members of all committees shall enter upon their duties immediately upon their appointment.

ARTICLE III—NOMINATION AND ELECTION OF OFFICERS

- **Section 1.** All persons seeking nomination for office in this department shall be required to submit their request in writing at the General Church Executive Board meeting in December prior to the general election in June.
- **Section 2.** In the event that only one nomination for an office is received, the nominated person shall be seated in that position.
- **Section 3.** Nomination for office shall be limited to bonafide members of the general department.
- **Section 4.** Only those who are paid up members shall be qualified to vote.

The General Young People's Department

ARTICLE I—NAME

This organization shall be known as the General Young People's Department of the United American Free Will

Baptist Denomination, Inc.

ARTICLE II—OBJECTIVES
A) To provide vital religious information that will stimulate a program of valuable experience for better living in a rapidly changing society.
B) To promote such a program within the denomination as to invigorate Christian interest within our young people.
C) To acquaint young people with the values of the general knowledge, benefits, and advantages offered through the Bible.
D) To emphasize the worth of self as well as the importance of respect for human dignity and concern for the rights and well being of others as we relate religion to other discipline.
E) To strengthen the bonds of Christian unity and fellowship.
F) To be supportive of the leadership and programs of the denomination.

ARTICLE III—MEMBERSHIP
Any person can be a member of this Department upon payment of dues provided they are a bonafide member of a local Free Will Baptist Church in this denomination.

ARTICLE IV—OFFICERS
The officers of this organization shall be president, vice president, recording secretary, financial secretary, treasurer, reporter, chaplain, executive committee and a trustee board.

BY-LAWS

ARTICLE I—RULES OF ORDER

Section 1. Robert's Rules of Order shall be the authority on all questions of procedure not specifically stated in the constitution and by-laws.

ARTICLE II—DUTIES AND TERMS OF OFFICE

- **Section 1.** All officers shall hold office for a period of three years. In case of a vacancy, the president of the department shall have power to fill the unexpired term.
- **Section 2.** The president shall preside at all meetings. He shall appoint all committees and shall be an ex of ficio member of all committees.
- **Section 3.** The vice president shall assist the president and shall preside in the absence of or at the request of the president.
- **Section 4.** The recording secretary shall keep a true and accurate record of the proceedings of the Department, shall assist the president with
- secretarial assignments for programs and correspondence of the department and shall assist the financial secretary as necessary and upon request, for
- efficient department operations.
- **Section 5.** The financial secretary shall keep a true and accurate record of all finances of the department both of collections and expenditures, and shall write all orders on the treasurer.
- **Section 6.** The treasurer shall deposit all monies of the department giving receipts for the same. They shall pay out money only by written order bearing the signatures of both the financial secretary and president.
- **Section 7.** The trustee board shall manage all the

temporal concerns of the department. They shall guard all property owned by the department.

- **Section 8.** The Chaplain shall be responsible for the devotional exercises to be conducted at each regular meeting.
- **Section 9.** The Executive Committee shall have the authority to conduct all business which shall arise between regular meetings and make recommendations to be acted upon by the membership.

ARTICLE III—COMMITTEES

- **Section 1.** Special committees will be appointed by the president as they are needed.
- **Section 2.** Members of all committees shall enter upon their duties immediately upon their appointment.

ARTICLE IV—NOMINATION AND ELECTION OF OFFICERS

- **Section 1.** All persons seeking nomination for office in this department shall be required to submit their request in writing at the General Church Executive Board meeting in December prior to the general election in June.
- **Section 2.** In the event that only one nomination for an office is received, the nominated person shall be seated in that position.
- **Section 3.** Nomination for of five shall be limited to bonafide members of the General Department.
- **Section 4.** Only those who are paid up members shall be qualified to vote.

ARTICLE V—MEETINGS

- **Section 1.** There shall be at least one scheduled meeting annually.
- **Section 2.** Special meetings can be called when the president feels it is necessary.

ARTICLE VI—MEMBERSHIP DUES

- **Section 1.** Dues shall be affixed by the Executive Committee.

Ordinances of the Church
Ceremonies—Consecrations— Ordinations— Dedications
The Lord's Supper

(The Mothers shall be responsible for the preparation of the elements of the Lord's Supper— unleavened bread and unfermented fruit of the vine). The Mothers should be attired in white during this ceremony. The Communion Table shall be prepared with white covering and the elements shall be covered prior to serving. The Mothers shall prepare a vessel of water that those administering the sacraments may wash their hands as a symbol of sanctification. The minister may break bread while he gives the meaning of the Lord's broken body and lifts the cup as he refers to our Lord's shed blood. At the close of the sermon or Scripture lesson, or at any time that he may deem proper, the minister with any members present and with the deacons who are to participate, may gather around the table and bow with the whole congregation, and the following prayer, or an extemporaneous one, if preferred, may be offered.

"Almighty God, our Heavenly Father, we praise Thee for the great love expressed in the gift of Thy blessed Son, who suffered death on the cross for our redemption, and made there a full and sufficient sacrifice and satisfaction for the sins of the whole world, and did institute this blessed sacrament to be a perpetual memorial of His precious death until He comes again. We pray Thee that Thou will grant that we who receive these emblems of His broken body and shed blood, in remembrance of His death and passion may be partakers of the divine nature by faith in His precious blood, who in the same night that He was betrayed took bread and when He had given thanks, broke it and gave it to His disciples, saying, "Take, eat; this is my body, which is given for you, do this in remembrance of me.' Likewise He took the cup, and when He had given thanks, He gave it to them saying, 'Drink ye all of this; for this is my blood of the New Testament, which is shed for you, and for many, for the remission of sins.' Do this in remembrance of me." Amen.

(Here the minister may partake of the communion in both kinds himself, and deliver to the others around the table, after which a suitable song may be sung or soft music and all Christians present regardless of denomination, shall be invited to the table to commemorate together the death of their blessed Saviour. In the administration of the elements, the parties offering the bread to the participants may say:

"The body of our Lord Jesus Christ, which was given for thee, to preserve thee unto everlasting life. Take and eat this in remembrance that Christ died for thee, and feed on Him by faith with thanksgiving."

(And the one that delivereth the cup shall say:)

"The blood of our Lord Jesus Christ, which was shed for thee, preserve thee unto everlasting life. Drink this in remembrance of His shed blood, and be thankful and rejoice in Him."

(After all have partaken, the services may close with a prayer or song, or the benediction, or all of these.)
(We recommend that only unfermented grape juice shall be used in the celebration of the Lord's Supper in all of our churches.)

The minister shall read a lesson of his own selection from the Holy Scriptures after which he may address the congregation saying:

"Dearly Beloved: The last command of our risen Lord was to go into all the world and preach the Gospel to every creature. The Holy Spirit throughout the Book of the Acts enforced this command through the Apostles in relation to all who believed in Christ; therefore, it is our duty as possessors of His grace to conform to this therefore, it is our duty as possessors of His grace to conform to this Great Commission, both in the preaching of the Word and the administration of the ordinance of baptism as opportunity affords."

(At this point, let the candidates for baptism be invited to stand before the congregation, the minister addressing them saying:)

"Dearly Beloved: This act of yours, coming seeking baptism in the name of the Lord, is a public testimony of your professed subjection to Christ and your willingness to follow Him. But that you may further declare your determination to walk in the way of the Lord and in the faith of Christ, you shall in the presence of God and of this congregation, give answer to the following questions:

1. "Do you have faith in our Lord Jesus Christ?" Answer: "I have."
2. "Will you endeavor to walk in the fear of God and in the way of His commandments?' Answer: "I will endeavor to do so."
3. "Will you attend Divine services as opportunity affords, and contribute of your means for the

spread of the full Gospel?" Answer: "I will."

4. "Do you desire to be baptized in this faith?"
   Answer, "This is my desire."

(Here the minister shall proceed to administer the ordinance to the candidate, saying:)
"In obedience to the command of the Word of God, and according to your profession of faith, I now baptize you in the name of the Father, and of the Son, and of the Holy Ghost, in Jesus name. Amen."

(After the baptism of the candidate the congregation may sing a hymn, followed by a prayer and benediction by the minister or appropriate person.

Marriage Ceremony

(At the day and time appointed for Solemnization of Matrimony, the Persons to be married shall come into the body of the Church, or shall be ready in some proper house with their friends and neighbors; and there standing together the Man on the right hand, and the Woman on the left, the Minister shall say),
"DEARLY beloved, we are gathered together here in the sight of God, and in the face of this company, to join together this Man and this Woman in holy Matrimony, which is an honorable estate, instituted of God, signifying, unto us the mystical union that is betwixt Christ and his Church; which holy estate Christ adorned and beautified with his presence and first miracle that he wrought in Cana of Galilee, and is commended of Saint Paul to be honourable among all men: and therefore is not by any to be entered into unadvisedly or lightly; but reverently, discreetly, advisedly, soberly, and in

the fear of God. Into this holy estate these two persons present come now to be joined. If any man can show just cause, why they may not lawfully be joined together, let him now speak, or else hereafter forever hold his peace.

(And also speaking unto the Persons who are to be married, he shall say),
I REQUIRE and charge you both, as ye will answer at the dreadful day of judgment when the secrets of all hearts shall be disclosed, that if either of you know any impediment, why ye may not be lawfully joined together in Matrimony, ye do now confess it. For be ye well assured, that if any persons are joined together otherwise than as God's Word doth allow, their marriage is not lawful. (The Minister, if he shall have reason to doubt of the lawfulness of the proposed Marriage, may demand sufficient surety for his indemnification; but if no impediment shall be alleged or suspected the Minister shall say to the Man),
_____wilt
thou have this Woman to thy wedded wife, to live together after God's ordinance in the holy estate of Matrimony? Wilt thou love her, comfort her, honour, and keep her in sickness and in health; and, forsaking all others, keep thee only unto her, so long as ye both shall live?
(The Man shall answer), I Will.

(Then shall the Minister say unto the Woman,)
wilt thou have this Man to thy wedded husband, to live together after God's ordinance in thy holy estate of Matrimony? Wilt thou love him, comfort him, honour, and keep him in sickness and in health; and, forsaking all others, keep thee only unto him, so long as ye both shall live?
(The Woman shall answer,) I Will.
(Then shall the Minister say,)

148

WHO giveth this Woman to be married to this Man? (Then shall they give their troth to each other in this manner. The Minister, receiving the Woman at her father's or friend's hands, shall cause the Man with his right hand to take the Woman by her right hand, and to say after him as followeth),

I_____take Thee_____to my wedded wife, to have and to hold from this day forward, for better for worse, for richer for poorer, in sickness and in health, to love, and to cherish, 'till death us do part, according to God's holy ordinance; and thereto I plight thee my troth.

(Then shall they loose their hands; and the Woman with her right hand taking the Man by his right hand shall likewise say after the Minister:)

I_____take thee_____to my wedded husband, to have and to hold from this day forward, for better for worse, for richer for poorer, in sickness and health, to love, and to cherish, 'till death us do part, according to God's holy ordinance; and thereto I give thee my troth.

(Then shall they again loose their hands; and the Man shall give unto the Woman a Ring. And the Minister taking the Ring shall deliver it unto the Man, to put it upon the fourth finger of the Woman's left hand. And the Man holding the Ring there, and taught by the Minister, shall say), With this ring I thee wed; In the Name of the Father, and of the Son, and of the Holy Ghost. Amen.
(And, before delivering the Ring to the Man, the Minister may say as followeth.)
BLESS, O Lord, this ring, that he who gives it and she who

wears it may abide in thy peace, and continue in thy favour, unto their life's end; through Jesus Christ our Lord. Amen.
(If double ring ceremony, repeat the above statements)

(Then, the man leaving the Ring upon the fourth finger of the Woman's left hand, the Minister shall say,)
Let us pray.

(Then shall the Minister and the People, still standing say the Lord's Prayer.)
OUR Father, who art in heaven, Hallowed be thy name. Thy kingdom come. Thy will be done, on earth as it is in heaven. Give us this day our daily bread. And forgive us our trespasses, As we forgive those who trespass against us. And lead us not into temptation, But deliver us from evil. For thine is the kingdom, and the power, and the glory, forever and ever.
Amen.

(Then shall the Minister add)
O ETERNAL God, Creator and Preserver of all mankind, Giver of all spiritual grace, the Author of everlasting life; Send thy blessing upon these thy servants, this man and this woman, whom we bless in thy Name; that they, living faithfully together, may surely perform and keep the vow and covenant betwixt them made, (whereof this Ring given and received is a token and pledge,) and may ever remain in perfect love and peace together, and live according to thy laws; through Jesus Christ our Lord. Amen.

(The Minister may add one or both of the following Prayers)
O ALMIGHTY God, Creator of mankind, who only art the wellspring of life; Bestow upon these thy servants, if it be thy will, the gift and heritage of children, and grant that they may

see their children brought up in thy faith and fear, to the honour and glory of Thy Name; through Jesus Christ our Lord. Amen.

O GOD, who hast so consecrated the state of Matrimony that in it is signified and represented the spiritual marriage and unity betwixt Christ and his Church; Look mercifully upon these thy servants, that they may love, honour, and cherish each other, and so live together in faithfulness and patience, in wisdom and true godliness, that their home may be a haven of blessing and of peace; through the same Jesus Christ our Lord, who liveth and reigneth with thee and the Holy Spirit ever, one God, world without end. Amen.

(Then shall the Minister join their right hands together, and say),
THOSE whom God hath joined together let no man put asunder.

(Then shall the Minister speak unto the Company.)
FORASMUCH as_____and
_____ have consented together in holy wedlock, and have witnessed the same before God and this company, and thereto have given and pledged their troth, each to the other, and have declared the same by giving and receiving a ring, and by joining hands; I pronounce that they are Man and Wife, in the Name of the Father, and of the son, and of the Holy host. Amen.

(The Man and Wife kneeling, the Minister shall add this Blessing.)
GOD, the Father, God the Son, God the Holy Ghost, bless, preserve, and keep you; the Lord mercifully with his favour look upon you, and fill you with all spiritual benediction and

grace; that ye may so live together in this life, that in the world to come ye may have life everlasting. Amen.

The Laying of a Cornerstone

- A platform should be erected, and all rubbish removed from the place before the assembling of the congregation.
- Hymn—"How Firm a Foundation"
- Scripture—Isaiah 28:16; Psalm 118:23
- Prayer
- Hymn—"The Church's One Foundation"
- Words of Welcome
- Statement of Progress on Building and in Raising Funds Special Music—"Onward Christian Soldiers"
- Responsive Reading

Pastor—Therefore saith the Lord God, Behold I lay in Zion for a foundation a stone, a tried stone, a precious cornerstone, a sure foundation.

People—Wherefore also it is contained in the Scripture, Behold, I lay in Zion a chief cornerstone, elect, precious; and he that believeth on him shall not be confounded.

Pastor—The stone which the builders refused is become the head stone of the corner.

People—This is the Lord's doing; it is marvelous in our eyes.

Pastor—And ye are built upon the foundation of the apostles and prophets, Jesus Christ himself being the Chief cornerstone.

People—In whom all the building fitly framed together groweth unto a holy temple in the Lord.

Pastor—in whom ye also are builded together for a habitation of God through the spirit.

152

People—ye are a chosen generation, a holy nation, a peculiar people.

Pastor—That ye should shew forth the praises of him who hath called you out of darkness into his marvelous light.

Union—That our sons may be as plants grown up in their youth that our daughters may be as cornerstones. Happy is that people that is in such a case; yea, happy is that people whose God is the Lord.

Hymn—"Blest Be The Tie"

Closing Prayer and Benediction

Dedication of Church Buildings

The Prelude

A Hymn—"The Church's One Foundation The Call to Worship

Minister—Who shall ascend into the hill of the Lord? And who shall stand in his Holy place?

Congregation—He that hath clean hands and a pure heart. Who hath not lifted up his soul unto falsehood, And hath not sworn deceitfully.

Minister—He shall receive a blessing Jehovah, And righteousness from the God of his salvation. This is the generation of them that seek after him, That seek thy face even Jacob.

Congregation—Lift up your heads, O ye gates and be ye lifted up, ye everlasting doors; and the King of Glory shall come in.

Minister—Who is the King of Glory?

Congregation—The Lord of hosts; He is the King of Glory.

The Lord's Prayer

The Scripture Lesson—Psalm 84:1-4, 10-12. The minister addresses the Trustees: You have been selected by the members of this church to fill the responsible positions of trustees of the House of Worship now being dedicated to the service and worship of Almighty God. You will at all times when you represent this church, act on its behalf and for its welfare.

God's holy temple is a sacred place in which He is to be worshipped in the beauty of holiness and love. Nothing should enter this sacred place that would defile it.

Protect it at all times; preserve it for continual service; improve it as needs and opportunities arise. To you is committed the task of keeping it worthy of its title, The House of God.

From this time forth because of your authority, you will hold this property in trust for God and the church of Jesus Christ. May Christian faith and hope and love dwell in your hearts, and may the Holy Spirit guide and direct you in all the activities that fall within the sphere of your responsibility as the Board of Trustees.

The Trustee Covenant

We, the Board of Trustees of the church, do covenant with God and one another to discharge our duties faithfully and to hold this House of Worship and Trust, that it may, at all times, magnify the preaching of the Word of God and thus fulfill its mission in this community for all the purposes for which it is now being set apart.

The Act of the Dedication

Minister—To the glory of God the Father, to the honor of Jesus Christ, His only begotten Son, our Saviour and to the praise of the Holy Spirit our Comforter.

Congregation—we dedicate this house.

Minister—For worship in prayer and praise; For the preaching of the word; For the celebration of the Holy Sacraments.

Congregation—we dedicate this house.

Minister—For comfort to those who mourn; For strength to those who are weak; For help to those who are tempted.

Congregation—we dedicate this house.

Minister—For the sanctity of the family; For the purity and guidance of childhood; For the promotion of brotherhood.

Congregation—we dedicate this house.

Minister—For promoting Christian patriotism; For developing a moral conscience; For the suppression of evil in all forms and everywhere; For the coming of the Kingdom of God on earth. Congregation—we dedicate this house.

Prayer of Dedication

"Almighty and Everlasting God, Thou dwellest not in temples made with hands, neither art Thou worshipped with men's hands, as though thou needest anything, seeing that Thou givest to all life and breath and all things; when we bring Thee our best, we serve Thee only with what is Thine own; and we have done all, we are but unprofitable servants. Yet do Thou, O Lord, who delightest Thyself in the praises of the sanctuary, accept the offering of this house which Thy people have builded to the glory of Thy Holy Name.

"We consecrate it to Thee, the Father, the Son, and the Holy Spirit, to be henceforth the House of God, and a gate of heaven; we set it apart from all common and worldly uses, for a temple and a sanctuary, where Thy holy gospel shall be preached; where the prayers of the church shall be made unto thee without ceasing; where Thy high praises shall be devoutly sung; where the ordinances of Thy Word shall be duly administered; to which Thy people shall throng with cheerful steps.

"When Thy gospel is preached in this place may it be spoken in the demonstration of the Spirit and with power. When Thy holy sacraments are administered, may those spiritual graces, which the outward signs do represent and signify, flow into the hearts of Thy servants. Here let God be worshipped in spirit and in truth. Here when Thy people come to offer their gifts upon Thine altar, may they consider him, who though he was right for our sakes became poor, that we through His poverty might be made rich. Let the glory of the Lord fill this house and the spirit of God descend and dwell in His church. Amen."

Hymn—"I Love Thy Kingdom, Lord"
An Offering
The Sermon
The Benediction

Dedication of Infants

At any regular church service, one may use a service of dedication for babies. During the singing of a hymn, ask the parents to come forward with their little ones and occupy the front seats. After a few words to the parents and the congregation as to the meaning and purpose of the service, ask this question of the parents: "Do you solemnly promise before God and these witnesses that you will, to the best of your ability, bring up this little one in the way of the Lord, making use of all the helps that God has given you in family religion, in church and Sunday school?" Parents should answer, "I do."

"To you the father, I give this red flower (rose or carnation) as a symbol of the rich red blood with which you build and defend the home into which this little one has come. May it be a home built firmly upon the ideals of Jesus, the man of Galilee, and the Son of God. Let nothing enter your home that will tend to destroy the faith, confidence and mutual love without which no home can long endure. Let nothing enter your home that will injure the soul of a little child, or crowd out the master who said, 'Whosever shall receive one of such children in my name receiveth me.' "To you the mother, I give this white flower (rose or carnation) as a symbol of the purity of heart and purpose with which you have endowed the home into which this little one has come. If your child grows up to know God as a personal experience, it will be largely because you have awakened the child's latent faith into its first consciousness of God, and because you have nurtured it in the things of God. It is from you, the greatest object in the child's affection, that the child gets its first idea of God. As you bow with the little one at your knee, the sense of awe and reverence is awakened in the little soul. "To you (use name of child), I give this small white flower (sweet pea) as a token of your innocency and purity of soul in the sight of God. My earnest prayer, as I look into your unsullied face, is that when you lose your irinocency, and your eyes of understanding are opened, you will see Jesus, whom to see is life and life eternal."

Prayer

"Our Father who art in heaven, Hallowed be thy name. Thy kingdom come. Thy will be done, on earth as it is in heaven. Give us this day our daily bread. And forgive us our trespasses, As we forgive those who trespass against us. And lead us not into temptation, But deliver us from evil. For thine is the kingdom, and the power, and the glory, forever and ever. Amen."

Ordination of Deacons

(When the time appointed by the bishop or Pastor is come, there shall be a sermon, or exhortation, declaring the duty and office of such as come to be ordained deacons; how necessary that order is in the Church of Christ, and also, how the people ought to esteem them in their office. The sermon being ended, a deacon shall present unto the bishop or pastor such as desire to be ordained deacons, each of them being decently dressed saying these words:)

"Honorable Bishop or Pastor, I present unto you these persons present, to be ordained deacons."

The Bishop or Pastor—Charge to the Church (Congregation Standing)

"Do you, the members of this Church, having sought divine guidance, choose the brethren standing before me to serve as deacons, and promise to give them honor, encouragement, and hearty support in the discharge of their duties?
Answer—"We do."

The Bishop or Pastor—Charge to the Deacons

"As you are about to enter upon your duties, we may be permitted to allude to the honor conferred upon you by your brethren, and express the hope that you will prove yourselves worthy of the confidence placed in you.
Never forget that, though partly concerned with temporalities, yours is a sacred office, and under the guidance and supervision of the elders, as far as lies in your

power, you will assist them in the responsible duty of shepherding the flock. We would remind you that the Scriptures say that they who use the office of a deacon well purchase to themselves a good degree, and great boldness in the faith which is in Jesus Christ. In all your labors we would commend you to God and to the Word of His Grace, which is able to build you up, and to give you an inheritance among the saints."

The Question (Bishop of Pastor)

Do you accept the of five of deacon in this church and promise that you will faithfully endeavor to discharge the duties thereof so as to promote the interests of the congregation and the cause of the truth and righteousness?

The Response by the Candidate

By the grace of God, I desire the of fine and will serve in meekness and love.

The Ordination Prayer

Most merciful Father we beseech Thee to send upon Thy servants Thy heavenly blessing, that they may be clothed with righteousness and have grace so to minister that Thy Church may be edified and strengthened in her holy life. Give them a large measure of the Spirit of Jesus, who came not to be ministered unto, but to minister. Make them strong to do Thy will, and give them great joy in their labors, to the honor of Thy Church and the glory of Thy name. Amen.

The Laying on of Hands

(The Bishop or Pastor appointed to ordain shall anoint with oil and lay hands reverently on each deacon, saying the following words. Likewise the elders or other ordained deacons shall follow, laying hands silently upon each candidate.)

"Brother, as you have been chosen by the members of your church to serve as a deacon, we confirm the office, and now ordain you to the office of deacon in the church of our Lord Jesus Christ, which He purchased by His own blood."

The Blessing (Bishop or Pastor)

"The Lord bless you and keep you.
The Lord make His face to shine upon you and be gracious unto you.
The Lord lift up the light of His countenance upon you and give you peace, in Jesus name. Amen."

Consecration of Mothers

(Candidates either standing or seated before the Bishop or Pastor)

An Introductory Word

You have been called to share in the greatest work of the church. Yours is the high honor of leading women to a richer and fuller life through Christian service. No nobler task could be given you. With every high privilege there are corresponding obligations. It is especially so in your case. You are also responsible for the preparation of the elements of the Lord's Supper.

You are entrusted with special duties. Your life, your words, your attitude, may influence many.

Your supreme duty is, through your leadership, to exalt Christ and thus to inspire those who follow your leadership and who give themselves to the service of God and their comrades. You are asked therefore to pledge your acceptance of these responsibilities.

To the Mothers

Do you accept this responsibility in earnestness and prayer? Do you affirm your purpose to lend a spirit of cooperation in every possible way; to be in your place of duty unless illness or other emergency prevents; to continually strive to grow in effectiveness through study and prayer; and to live such a life that your influence will lead others to the service of Christ?
If you accept these obligations, please signify by saying, "I do." Answer: "I Do."

The Charge

Mothers—you have accepted the responsibility of your position. You are charged therefore to keep in mind the challenge of the task you are committed.

I charge you to study. Show yourselves approved; workmen that have no cause for shame. I charge you to pray. Pray without ceasing. Sit often at the feet of the Master, learn of Him how to pray, how to live, how to lead. I charge you to keep ever before you the ultimate goal of all your efforts, the uniting of women around the world in the service of Christ. You are to inspire sacrificial service. You are to help bring the Kingdom of God in its fullness, and to speed the day when God's will shall be done on earth as it is in heaven. You are to assist at the Lord's Supper Table. You are to train the young women to love, honor, and respect their husbands. Their husbands are the head of the house as Christ is the head of the Church.

Let us Pray: (The Prayer of Consecration)

The Anointing With Oil

(All other regular Mothers should stand and take part in this service as well as ordained deacons. Candidates should kneel while the prayer of consecration is being made. They should stand or sit for the anointing with oil. After the completion of the ceremony, the regular Mothers should escort these candidates to their seats.)

Ordination of Ministers, Bishop or Elder

Brethren, these are they whom we purpose, God willing, this day to Ordain Elders: For after due examination, we find not the contrary, but that they are lawfully called to this function and Ministry; and that they are persons meet for the same. But, if there be any of you knoweth of any impediment or crime in any of them, for the which he ought not to be received into this Holy Ministry, let him come forth in the name of God and show what the crime or impediment is.

The Collect

Almighty God, giver of all good things, Who by the Holy Spirit has appointed Divers orders in Ministers in Thy church, mercifully behold these thy servants now called to the of five of Elders, and replenish them with the innocency of life, that both by word and good example they may faithfully serve Thee in this office to the Glory of Thy name and the edification of Thy Church, Who liveth and reigneth with Thee and the Holy Ghost, world without end. Amen.

Unto every one of us is given grace according to the measure of the gift of Christ. Wherefore He saith, when He ascended up on high, He led captivity captive, and gave gifts unto men. (Now that He has ascended what is it but that He also descended first into the lower parts of the earth? He that descended is the same also that ascended up far above all heavens, that He might fill all things.)

And He also gave some, Apostles; and some, prophets; and some, Evangelists; and some, Pastors and teachers; for the perfecting of the Saints, for the work of the Ministry, for the edifying of the body of Christ: Till we all come in the unity of Faith, and of Knowledge of the Son of God, unto a perfect man, unto the measure of the stature of the fullness of Christ.

Verily, verily, I say unto you, he that entereth not by the door into the sheepfold, but climbeth in some other way, the same is a thief and a robber.

But, he that entereth in by the door is the shepherd of the sheep. To him the porter openeth, and the sheep hear his voice; and he calleth his own sheep by name and leadeth him out. And when he putteth forth his own sheep, he goeth before them, and the sheep follow him for they know his voice. And a stranger will they not follow, but will flee from him, for they know not the voice of strangers. This parable spake Jesus unto thee, but they understood not what things they were which he spake unto them.

Bishop or Elder:

Then said Jesus unto them again, verily, verily, I say unto you, I am the door of the sheep.

All that ever came before me are thieves and robbers; but the sheep did not hear them. I am the door. By Me if any man enter in, he shall be saved and shall go in and out and find pasture.

The thief cometh not but for to steal, and to kill and to destroy; I am come that they might have life, and that they might have it more abundantly. I am the Good Shepherd; the Good Shepherd giveth His life of the sheep.

But he that is a hireling and not the Shepherd, whose own sheep are not, seeth the wolf coming and leaveth the sheep, and fleeth, and the wolf catcheth them, and scattereth the sheep. The hireling fleeth because he is a hireling and careth not for the sheep. I am the Good Shepherd and know My sheep, and I am known of mine. As the Father knoweth Me, even so I know the Father; and I lay down My life for the sheep. And other sheep I have which are not of this fold; them also I must bring, and they shall hear My voice, and there shall be one fold and one Shepherd.

Bishop or Elder:

You have heard brethren, as well in your private examinations as in the exhortation which was just made to you, and in the writing of the Apostles, of what dignity and how greatly important this office is, where unto ye are now called. And now again, we exhort you in the name of our Lord Jesus Christ that ye have in remembrance into how high a dignity and to how weighty an office ye are called; that is to say, to be messengers, watchmen, and stewards of the Lord; to teach and to adomish, to feed and to provide for the Lord's family; to seek for Christ's sheep that are dispersed abroad, and for His children who are in the midst of the evil world, that they may be saved through Christ forever.

We have good hope that you have weighed and pondered these things with yourself long before this time; and that you have clearly determined by God's Grace to give yourselves to this office, whereby it has pleased God to call you, so that as much as lieth in you, you will apply yourselves wholly to this one thing, and draw all cares and studies this way; that you will continually pray to God the Father, by the mediation of our Lord and only Saviour, Jesus Christ, for the Heavenly assistance of the Holy Ghost; that by daily reading and weighing the Scriptures, ye may wax riper and stronger in your ministry and that ye may so endeavor yourselves from time to time, to sanctify the Christ, that ye may be wholesome and goodly examples and patterns for the people to follow.

And now that this present congregation of Christ here assembled may also understand your minds and wills in these things; and that this your promise may move you more to do your duties. You shall answer plainly to these things which we, in the name of God and His Church shall demand to you, touching the same.

Bishop or Elder:

Do you think in your heart that you are truly called according to the will of Our Lord Jesus Christ, to the Order of Elder?

Candidates:

I do so believe.

Bishop or Elder:

Are you persuaded that the Holy Scriptures contain sufficiently all doctrine required of necessity for Eternal salvation through faith in Jesus Christ? Are you determined out of said Scriptures to instruct the people committed to your charge, and to teach nothing as required of necessity to Salvation, but that which ye shall be persuaded may be concluded and proved by the Scriptures?

Candidates

I am so persuaded, and have so determined by God's Grace.

Bishop or Elder:

Will you then give your faithful diligence always to Minister the doctrine and Sacraments and Discipline of Christ as the Lord hath commended?

Candidates:

I will do so, by the help of the Lord.

Bishop or Elder:

Will you be ready with all faithful diligence always to banish and drive away all erroneous and strange doctrines contrary to God's Word; and to use both public and private monitions and exhortations, as well as the at sick as to the whole within your charge as need shall be required and occasion shall be given?

Candidates:

I will, the Lord being my helper.

Bishop or Elder:

Will you be diligent in prayer and in reading the Holy Scriptures, and in such studies as help to the knowledge of the same, laying aside the study of the world and of the flesh?

Candidates:

I shall apply myself thereto—the Lord being my helper.

Bishop or Elder:

Will you maintain and set forth, as much as lieth in you,

sweetness, peace and love among all Christian People, and especially among them that are, or shall be committed, to your charge?

Candidates:
I will do so, the Lord being my helper.

Bishop or Elder:
Will you reverently obey your chief ministers unto whom is committed the charge and government over you, Following with a glad mind and will their Godly Admonitions, submitting yourselves to their Godly judgments?

Candidates:
I will do so, the Lord being my helper.

Bishop or Elder:
Almighty God, who hath given you this will to do all these things, Grant also unto you strength and power to perform the same; That He may accomplish His work which He hath begun, Through JESUS CHRIST OUR LORD. AMEN.
(At this point the anointing with oil and the laying on of hands.)

The Burial of the Dead

(The minister at the house or church may read the following Scripture:)

Psalm 39: "I said, I will take heed to my ways, that I sin not with my tongue: I will keep my mouth with a bridle, while the wicked is before me, I was dumb with silence, I held my peace, even from good; and my sorrow was stirred. My heart was hot within me, while I was musing the fire burned: then spake I with my tongue, LORD make me to know mine end, and the measure of my days, what it is; that I may know how frail I am. Behold, thou hast made my days as an handbreath; and mine age is as nothing before thee: verily every man at his best state is altogether vanity. Selah.Surely they are disquieted in vain: he heapeth up riches, and knoweth not who shall gather them. And now, Lord, what wait I for? my hope is in thee. Deliver me from all my transgressions: make me not the reproach of the foolish. I was dumb, I opened not my mouth; because thou didst it. Remove thy stroke away from me: I am consumed by the blow of thine hand. When thou with rebukes dost correct man for iniquity, thou makest his beauty to consume away like a moth: surely every man is vanity. Selah. Hear my prayer, O LORD and give ear unto my cry; hold not thy peace at my tears: for I am a stranger with thee, and a sojourner, as all my fathers were. "O spare me, that I may recover strength before I go hence, and be no more."

(At the grave when the corpse is laid in the earth the minister shall say:)

"I am the resurrection, and the life: he that believeth in me,
....
shall never die" (John 11:25, 26).

"For I know that my redeemer liveth, and that he shall stand at the latter day upon the earth: And though after my skin worms destroy this body, yet in my flesh shall I see God; Whom I shall see for myself, and mine eyes shall behold, and not another" (Job 19:25-27).

("We brought nothing into this world and it's certain we can carry nothing out.") The LORD gave, and the LORD hath taken away; blessed be the name of the LORD" (Job 1:21).

"Here is the patience of the saints: here are they that keep the commandments of God, and the faith of Jesus. And I heard a voice from heaven saying unto me, Write, Blessed are the dead which die in the Lord from henceforth; Yea, saith the Spirit, that they may rest from their labours; and their works do follow them" (Revelation 14:12-13).

"Man that is born of woman hath but a short time to live and is full of misery. He cometh up and is cut down like a flower; he fleeth as it were a shadow, and never continue in one stay. In the midst of life there is death; of whom may we seek for succor, but of thee, O Lord, who for our sins art justly displeased? Yet, O Lord, God, most holy, O Lord most mighty, O holy and merciful Saviour, deliver us not into the bitter pains of eternal death. Thou knowest Lord the secret of hearts; Shut not thy merciful ears to our prayers, but spare us. Lord most holy, O God most mighty, O holy and merciful Saviour, thou most worthy judge eternal, suffer us not at our last hour for any pains of death to fall from thee."

(Then shall the minister say:) "Forasmuch as it hath pleased Almighty God in his wise providence, to take out of this world the soul of the departed, we therefore commit the body to the ground; earth to earth, ashes to ashes, dust to dust; looking for the general resurrection in the last day, and the life of the world to come, through our Lord Jesus Christ; at whose Second Coming in glorious majesty, to judge the world, the earth and sea shall give up their dead, and the corruptible bodies of those who sleep in him shall be changed and made like unto his glorious body, according to the mighty working whereby he is able to subdue ail things unto himself. I heard a voice from heaven saying unto me, Write, from henceforth blessed are the dead which died in the Lord, even so saith the spirit, they rest from their labors. Lord have mercy on us. Christ have mercy on us. Lord have mercy on us."

(Let us pray:)

"Our Father who art in heaven, Hallowed be thy name. Thy kingdom come. Thy will be done, on earth as it is in heaven. Give us this day our daily bread. And forgive us our trespasses, As we forgive those who trespass against us. And lead us not into temptation, But deliver us from evil. For thine is the kingdom, and the power, and the glory, forever and ever. Amen."

Formal Letters

Form of Letter From an Annual Convention to the
U.A.F.W.B. General Conference

To the U.A.F.W.B. General Conference to be held with the church at _____ in the county of _____ and state of _ the _____ Convention is again blessed to make its triennial report, as follows:

Received _____

Dismissed _____

Expelled _____

Died In _____

Total Number of Members _____

Number of Auxiliaries Added _____

Total Number of Auxiliaries _____

Total Number of Members _____

Total Amount Raised _____

Total Amount Paid for Budget _____

Representing to the General Conference with

_____

Balance on Hand _____

_____

President

_____

Delegate

_____

Formal Letter From An Auxiliary

To the Annual Convention

To the Annual Convention to be held with

_____

We the members of_____

are again blessed to make our annual report as follows:

Received_____

Dismissed _____

Expelled _____

Died _____

Total Number of Members _____

Total Amount of Money Raised During the Year _____

Amount Paid Sick _____

Amount of Budget Given _____

Amount of Budget Sent to the Convention _____

Amount of Money on Hand _____

We Send _____

Delegates

_____

President

_____

Secretary

_____

Pastor

_____

Y.P.C.L. Letter to a Convention

To the_____Convention, to be
held with the_____F.W.B. Church, in the
county of_____and state of_____.
We the members request permission to make the following
annual report:
Received _____
Baptized _____
Added by Letter _____
Dismissed _____
Expelled _____
Deceased _____
Total Members _____
Budget _____
Amount Paid _____
Amount Raised _____
Do you wish the next Convention? _____
Time of Meetings _____

Name of Delegate

_____

Delegate

_____

Secretary

_____

Formal Letter

From a Church to the Annual Conference

To the_____Conference, to be held with the

church at_____, in the county of_, state of

_____.

We, the members of_____church, in the county of_____,

are again blessed to make our annual report as follows:

Received_____

Baptized _____

Added by Letter _____

Dismissed _____

Expelled _____

Died _____

Total members _____

Value of Church Property _____

Budget Money _____

Amount Paid Our Pastor _____

Time of Quarterly Meeting _____

Pastor for the Next Year _____

We Send

_____

Delegate, Please give our church the conference next year.

_____Secretary

of Said Church

_____

Pastor

_____

A Letter From an Annual Conference to the General Conference Name of Annual

Name of Annual Conference_____

	20__	20__	20__
Received			
Baptized			
Added by Letter			
Dismissed			
Expelled			
Exempted			
Died			
Churches Added			
Churches Dismissed			
Churches Excluded			
Ministers Licensed			
Ministers Ordained			
Net Increase or Decrease of Members			
Number of Churches			
Number of Members			
Number of Licentiates			
Number of Elders			
General Funds Raised			
Value of Church Property			
Budget to General Conference			

Delegates to the General Conference

Letter of Dismission

This certifies that___is a regular member of
_____ a U.A.F.W.B. Church in
_____County, and state of
_____, in good standing.
We recommend
_____ to the fellowship of God's people, and
when we are informed that_____has united with another
evangelical church, we shall consider
_____regularly dismissed from this church.

This letter is written on behalf of the United American Free
Will Baptist Church in_____.

_____
Secretary

_____
Pastor

A Transfer

This certifies that the bearer,_____

_____has

transferred from_____Annual

Conference to_____ Annual

Conference. This minister is in good standing, and is

recommended to your fellowship.

Ministerial Certificate

This bearer of this certificate:_____has

given evidence of God's call into the Gospel Ministry, and is

permitted to exercise this gift as opportunities arise under

the supervision of the pastor of

their membership church.

Preacher's License

This certifies that the bearer_____,

of the United American Free Will Baptist Church, at_____

_____in the County of_____,

State of _____having been divinely called, and after

due proof of their efficiency by us, and in testimony of our

approval, is commissioned to preach the Gospel

of our Lord and Saviour, and is hereby commended to the

fellowship of all Christians. In behalf of Annual Conference.

Credentials

This certifies that the bearer,_____of the
County of

_____, State of_____, a worthy
member of_____ Conference has this day been publicly
ordained to the work of the Christian Ministry by fasting and
prayer and the laying on of the hands of the Presbytery,
according to the usage of the U.A.F.W.B. Denomination, and
is hereby authorized to preach the Gospel and administer its
Ordinances wherever the Great Deity in His providence
may call.

(Transfer) Credentials

This certifies that the bearer,_____of
the County of

_____

State of,_____a worthy member of_____

_____

Conference has this day been commissioned to the work of
the Christian Ministry according to the usage of the
U.A.F.W.B. Denomination, Inc., and is hereby authorized to
preach the Gospel and administer its Ordinances wherever
the Great Deity in His providence may so call.

Ministerial Certificate of Approval

This is to certify that _____
is a minister in full fellowship with his church and
conference, and is therefore recommended for all
ministerial privileges and rights as applicable.

*(All preceding licenses/ certificates are valid for one year,
and subject to yearly renewal)*

Form of Missionary Certificate

To Whom It May Concern:
This certifies that the bearer _____, of the
County of _____, and the State of_____,
a worthy member of the United American Free Will Baptist
Church, at _____, has this day been publicly set
apart to do the work for the Home Mission Department of the
U.A.F.W.B. Church by the board of trustees of the Annual
Convention of the above named department, and is
authorized to lecture on missionary work and to solicit aid to
advance upon the condition that all money or valuables
given shall be accounted for. Any default will subject the
bearer to indictment before civil laws; and if upon trial, is
found guilty, this certificate is revoked, and the offender left
to the discretion of the court. I hereby accept the above
indenture.

_____

Missionary

Formal Letter From an Annual Convention to the U.A.F.W.B. General Conference

To the U.A.F.W.B. General Conference to be held with the church at_____ in the county of_____and state of

_____ the_____Convention is again blessed to make its triennial report, as follows:

Received_____

Dismissed _____

Expelled _____

Died In _____

Total Number of Members _____

Number of Auxiliaries Added _____

Total Number of Auxiliaries _____

Total Number of Members _____

Total Amount Raised _____

Total Amount Paid for Budget _____

Representing to the General Conference with _____

Balance on Hand _____

_____

Delegate

_____

Secretary

_____

President

www.ingramcontent.com/pod-product-compliance
Lightning Source LLC
Chambersburg PA
CBHW062055270326
41931CB00013B/3091